Paul-Marie of the Cross, OCD

Carmelite Spirituality in the Teresian Tradition

About the Author

Paul-Marie of the Cross, OCD, was born Paul Hayaux du Tilly in Paris in 1902. He studied at the Sorbonne and the Institute Catholique. He was ordained a diocesan priest of Paris in 1933, and served as the assistant director of the Ecole Gerson before entering the Discalced Carmelites in 1941. As a Carmelite, he became director of the college of St. Thérèse at Avon after the arrest of Père Jacques. He was later prior of the Carmelite monastery at Lille, and in charge of the Écoles d'Oraison Carmélitaines. He died in 1975. Among his many writings are The Biblical Spirituality of St. John *(Staten Island, NY: Alba House, 1966) and* The Spiritual Message of the Old Testament, *3 vols. (St. Louis, MO: B. Herder Book Co., 1961–1963).*

Paul-Marie of the Cross, OCD

Carmelite Spirituality in the Teresian Tradition

Translated by Kathryn Sullivan, RSCJ

*Revised and edited with a Preface
by Steven Payne, OCD*

ICS Publications
Institute of Carmelite Studies
Washington, D.C.
1997

The French version of this essay originally appeared in *La Spiritualité Catholique,* ed. Jean Gautier (Paris: Le Rameau, 1953), and was translated into English by Kathryn Sullivan, RSCJ, as the article "Carmelite Spirituality" in *Some Schools of Catholic Spirituality,* ed. Jean Gautier (New York: Desclée, 1959). The present revised version is edited from Kathryn Sullivan's 1959 translation, with her permission.

Graphics on pages 16 and 83, and between pages 68 and 69, are by Robert F. McGovern. Cover design by Nancy Gurganus of Grey Coat Graphics.

ICS Publications
2131 Lincoln Road NE
Washington, DC 20002-1199
800-832-8489

Typeset and produced in the U.S.A.

Library of Congress Cataloging-in-Publication Data

Paul Marie, de la Croix.
   Carmelite spirituality in the Teresian tradition /
   Paul-Marie of the Cross, OCD;
translated by Kathryn Sullivan; revised and edited with a preface by
Steven Payne.
     p. cm.
   Includes bibliographical references.
    ISBN: 0-935216-50-2
   1. Carmelites—Spiritual Life. 2. Spirituality—Catholic Church
—History. I. Payne, Steven, 1950-. II. Title.
BX3203.P38   1997
248.8'94—dc20   94-27728
                                     CIP

TABLE OF CONTENTS

ABBREVIATIONS

In this essay, Père Paul-Marie quotes Carmelite authors extensively, from the older editions available to him, sometimes without indicating the exact source of particular passages. Wherever the source could be identified more precisely, we have supplied the reference and updated the quotations to correspond with current translations available from ICS Publications and others. Otherwise we have left the quotations as they appeared in Sr. Kathryn Sullivan's original translation (except for minor editing).

Thus, all quotations from **St. John of the Cross** that include an indication of the source are taken from *The Collected Works of St. John of the Cross,* trans. Kieran Kavanaugh and Otilio Rodriguez, rev. ed. (Washington, DC: ICS Publications, 1991). For his major works, the following abbreviations are used:

Ascent = Ascent of Mount Carmel
Canticle = Spiritual Canticle
Flame = Living Flame of Love
Night = Dark Night

In references to the *Ascent* and *Night,* the first number indicates the book. Also, references to John's *Poems, Letters,* and *Sayings* are based on the numbering in this revised Kavanaugh/Rodriguez translation, which sometimes differs from that of other editions.

Similarly, all quotations from **St. Teresa of Jesus** that include a source reference are taken from *The Collected Works of St. Teresa of Avila,* trans. Kieran Kavanaugh and Otilio Rodriguez, 3 vols. (Washington, DC: ICS Publications, 1976–1985). For her major works, the following abbreviations are used:

Castle = Interior Castle
Foundations = Book of Foundations
Life = Book of Her Life
Way = Way of Perfection

In references to the *Castle,* the first number refers to the "dwelling places."

Insofar as possible, all quotations from **Brother Lawrence, Thérèse of Lisieux,** and **Elizabeth of the Trinity** are taken from the ICS translations of their works, listed in the bibliography at the end of this volume. References to Brother Lawrence include the title of the section and the paragraph numbering in the ICS edition. References to Bl. Elizabeth and St. Thérèse give the page number in the ICS editions. References to the letters of Thérèse and Elizabeth are also indicated by "LT" and "L" respectively, together with the number of the letter in the ICS editions, which follow the numbering in the critical French editions.

Finally, as is well known, early editions of St. Thérèse's *l'Histoire d'une Âme* [Story of a Soul] were extensively edited by her sister Pauline (Mother Agnes), and included a section of "Counsels and Reminiscences" not found in the later critical edition. In some cases, where Fr. Paul-Marie quotes from this section and the equivalent passage could not be easily located in current editions, we have used the English translation found in *Soeur Thérèse of Lisieux, the Little Flower of Jesus: A New and Complete Translation of l'Histoire d'une Âme...,* trans. Thomas N. Taylor (New York: P. J. Kenedy & Sons, 1912). These few quotations are indicated by the word *Counsels,* together with the page number in the Taylor translation on which the text appears.

Preface to the Revised Edition

The Carmelite tradition is far less a matter of doctrines and ideas than the story of a vibrant spiritual family, a particular movement of the Spirit of Jesus among God's people. Therefore, as the author of this work admits at the outset, any attempt to summarize briefly the whole range of Carmelite spirituality seems foolhardy at best. Few, in fact, have even tried, and fewer still have succeeded as brilliantly. In less than 100 pages, and in his characteristically vivid style, the late Paul-Marie of the Cross manages to touch on Carmel's origins, the spirit of her Rule, her Elijan and Marian heritage, the legacy of Teresa of Avila and John of the Cross, the modern contribution of Thérèse of Lisieux and others, and the Carmelite understanding of prayer and contemplation.

This article began as a contribution to Jean Gautier's French anthology, *La Spiritualité Catholique* (Paris: Le Rameau, 1953), a volume later translated into English by Sr. Kathryn Sullivan, RSCJ, as *Some Schools of Catholic Spirituality* (Paris: Desclée, 1959). Long out of print, Père Paul-Marie's essay nevertheless remains a favorite among Discalced Carmelites, and is still read in many formation programs as one of the best brief introductions to the Carmelite tradition.

Naturally, any text bears the marks of the period and context in which it was composed, and the present essay, written from the perspective of a Discalced Carmelite friar of the 1950s, is no exception. To the essay's original title, "Carmelite Spirituality," we have therefore added "in the Teresian Tradition," to acknowledge that this work represents the classical view of the Carmelite heritage particularly among the spiritual daughters and sons of St. Teresa of

Avila. Other approaches are certainly possible. Carmelites writing today would perhaps have more to say about other aspects of the Rule (e.g., the communitarian dimension), other members of the broader Carmelite family (including the large number of affiliated religious communities and lay Carmelites), and other important Carmelite figures who have come to prominence more recently, such as Titus Brandsma, Edith Stein, Raphael Kalinowski, and Teresa of the Andes. Readers wanting to know more about any of these may consult some of the works listed in the bibliography added for this edition.

Again, new historical research has begun elucidating, and sometimes correcting, earlier accounts of the origins of Carmel and of the Teresian Reform. Scholars now recognize, for example, that the Teresian Carmel arose not so much in reaction against the supposed "decadence" of its parent Order, but out of a Castilian Carmelite province already considered "observant." In a few sections, therefore, I have slightly amended Père Paul-Marie's text or added notes to bring his essay more into line with contemporary historical findings.

Nevertheless, this study has aged remarkably well, partly because the author focuses so much on the perennial themes of Carmelite spirituality. I have tried in this edition to preserve as much as possible the content of Père Paul-Marie's original presentation as well as the flavor of Sr. Kathryn Sullivan's fine translation, editing only lightly to bring some of the punctuation, vocabulary, spelling, and citations up to date. I wish to thank both Sr. Kathryn and Desclée for their cooperation in this project.

To most readers, ICS Publications is best known for providing contemporary English-language editions of Teresa of Avila, John of the Cross, Thérèse of Lisieux, and other major figures of the Carmelite tradition (such as Brother Lawrence, Elizabeth of the Trinity, and Edith Stein). In recent years, however, there have been a growing number of requests that we continue expanding our offerings to include shorter introductions, commentaries, and new editions of significant out-of-print works on the whole range of Carmelite themes. We hope therefore that this reprint edition will find for Père Paul-Marie's essay a new and enthusiastic audience.

Steven Payne, OCD

Introduction

The Order of Our Lady of Mount Carmel counts among its members many mystics and many saints, its roots are plunged deep in the Old Testament, its mission is specifically spiritual, and yet at no time in the past does it seem to have made any special effort to define its spirituality. Doesn't this make the present work presumptuous?

It is true that the members of the "Carmelite family" feel closely united to one another by "a characteristic and permanent way of seeing, feeling, willing."[1] It is also true that Carmel possesses texts that are especially representative of its traditions and spirit, but these texts are rather like reminders or manifestations than sources.

To characterize the spirituality of Carmel is all the more difficult because unlike other religious families Carmel has, in the strict sense of the word, no *founder* who trained it or gave it a rule. As a matter of fact no rule was written until the hermits of Mount Carmel requested one. And this was but the codification of the form of life that they had spontaneously adopted.

Where are the sources of Carmel's spirit to be found and how can that spirit be acquired?

To answer these questions, two things are necessary. First, we must understand the nature of this *spirit,* which came down from heaven upon the *sons of the prophets* dwelling century after century on the slopes of the holy mountain, because without this spirit Carmel would never have started and would never have lasted. We must also grasp the extraordinary signs of this spirit that are evident in those who possess it and give it full expression.

We will see that Carmelite spirituality is based only in part on documents. It is above all *spirit and life*. So it follows that by examining its origins and searching the Rule, as well as the lives and writings of the Order's great saints, that the soul of Carmel is revealed and, at the same time, Carmelite spirituality is made manifest.

The frontispiece of Alonso de Jesús María's *Doctrina de Religiosos* (1613) shows Mary in the Carmelite habit, spreading her protective mantle over the Order. St. Joseph stands behind her and Elijah kneels at the far left.

I. The Sources

Elijah the Prophet

Although it is certain that "schools [or guilds] of prophets" [cf. 1 Kgs 20:35; 2 Kgs 2:3–15; 4:38; 5:22; 6:1; 9:1] were established on Mount Carmel in the footsteps of Elijah and Elisha, it is impossible to discover how and when these schools became permanent institutions. Despite the mystery of these beginnings Carmel has always claimed Elijah as its own and has seen in him one who inaugurated the eremitic and prophetic life that is its characteristic.

This is not to say that Elijah introduced within the Old Testament frame of reference a special spirit, a new doctrine, a personal *way*. On the contrary, Elijah is typical of the prophets and just men and women who lived under the Old Covenant. But his disciples remembered this distinguishing note about him: he is the man whom the Spirit of Yahweh led into deep solitude and who, drawing waters from the "torrent of Carith," drank from the rivers of living water and tasted, in contemplation, *pleasures that are divine.* Therefore, if it is in documents that we wish to find the spirit of Carmel it is to the chapters in the first book of Kings dealing with this prophet that we must go.

Here in fact rings out that fundamental note that will reecho down the centuries, not only in the rocky solitudes of Mount Carmel but throughout the whole history of the Order. In Elijah, Carmel sees itself as in a mirror. His eremitic and prophetic life expresses its own most intimate ideal. In studying the life of Elijah, Carmel is aware of a growing thirst for contemplation. It perceives its deep kinship with this man who "stood in the presence of the living God." If it shares his weaknesses and his anguish, it also knows his faith in God and his zeal for the "Yahweh of armies" [1 Kgs 19:10, 14], the Lord of Hosts, and it has tasted the same delights of a life hidden in God that the prophet also experienced. When it discovers in the light of the inspired word that Elijah, "in the strength he drew from the divine food, walked forty days and forty nights to Horeb, the mountain of God" [1 Kgs 19:8], it is not in the least surprised. How could the prophet not have been drawn to this spot where that tremendous event of the religious history of humanity had taken place several centuries earlier: God's revelation to Moses?

There, in the bleak wastes of Sinai, we read in the book of Exodus that Moses, silent and alone, perceived Yahweh's mysterious presence in the light of fiery flames that burned the bush without consuming it (Ex 3:2). There the incommunicable Name, the divine transcendence and benevolence, were revealed to him. There, Moses understood that he must make known to those entrusted to him what he had been allowed to contemplate. "Say this to the people of Israel: 'I AM has sent me to you'" (Ex 3:14).

How could the father of contemplative life not have been drawn to this mountain, where God spoke to Moses "as one speaks to a friend" (Ex 33:11), where a human being dared address this prayer to God: "show me thy glory" (Ex 33:18)? How could he have failed to see that all the elements essential to contemplation were already contained in the scene on Horeb? So we may say that having found its model in Elijah, Carmel advances with him toward the very origin of true contemplative life. Or, it might be more exact to say that having found the contemplative experience in its origin (carried by Elijah to the highest degree of purity, detachment, and fulfillment), the Carmelites, wishing to renew this experience, feel obliged to recreate in their souls the climate in which this life grew: the desert with its spiritual solitude and silence. And they, in their turn, feel constrained to undertake this persevering march toward the mountain of God where fire burns but does not consume.

Carmelite spirituality in every century needs to breathe the air of these high places if it is to live; and it needs a form of life sufficiently recollected to permit the soul to perceive the divine presence "in the sound of a gentle breeze" (cf. 1 Kgs 19:12). In this perpetual return to solitude and recollection, this nostalgic call to detachment—"I will allure her, and bring her into the wilderness, and speak to her heart" (Hos 2:14)—Carmelites find the very soul of their vocation.

So they take as guides those who have advanced along the paths of divine union and have tasted the sweetness of heavenly things; and they pray with Elisha to his father Elijah to grant them a double portion of his spirit (2 Kgs 2:9).

Can we describe this spirit?

In spite of the mystery of its beginnings, on this point no hesitation is possible. This spirit consists essentially in a longing for union with God.

It will be objected that all spiritual people know this longing. This is true. Nevertheless for Carmel this aspiration has a quality of immediacy, an insistence on prompt realization that distinguishes the Order's religious attitude.[2] Carmel makes contemplation its proper end, and to attain this end it practices absolute detachment in relation to all demands, or at least to all temporal contingencies. Eminently theocentric, Carmel refers itself wholly to the living God: "As the Lord the God of Israel lives, before whom I stand" (1 Kgs 17:1).

From the earliest ages union with God has been its *raison d'être* and its soul. No doubt it was the anticipation of the grace of the Savior that made this possible. No doubt, too, that it has benefited by the progress and development of revelation down the centuries. Nevertheless in Carmel from the beginning, union with God has been and continues to be central.

Characterized by an awareness of the presence within the human heart of the very being of God, the spirit of Carmel also includes a sense of the sacred and a thirst for things divine. Progress in the experience of God only serves to deepen and develop this basic and truly essential element. Without it neither the wise nor the simple could enter into and intensify their relations with God.

No matter how individual and difficult to analyze this spirit may be, it is to be identified with the most authentic mysticism. At Carmel nothing imitative or esoteric is to be found, and the Carmelite tradition is singularly sober as to the content of spiritual experiences, though their presence is frequently attested. Always objective, it merely affirms the possibility and the reality of direct contact with God and points out the necessity, if this is to be attained, of recourse to a particular kind of life—the eremitic life.

It assigns no date to its first manifestations but instead states forcefully that, granted certain conditions, it is possible for human beings truly to live the divine life. For this it suffices to realize in oneself the climate of the original desert, and after withdrawing into this interior solitude, "to hold oneself in the presence of the living God." Then the light of truth will come to purify, enlighten, and enkindle our souls.

Foundations are thus laid for a personal experience of God and the intimate relations that a creature may have with the Creator. Going back through the ages, Carmel will never hesitate to recognize itself in the first hermit whom the Bible describes for us, and to model its life on those vowed to the contemplation of divine things in silence and solitude.

Carmelites have traditionally seen the small cloud rising out of the sea, in response to Elijah's prayer on Carmel (cf. 1 Kgs 18:44), as a symbol of Mary.

II. Characteristics of Carmel

Primacy of the Contemplative Spirit

A direct and intimate experience of God is the basis of Carmelite spirituality. Therefore, before any Rule, and in order that the Rule may be lived when it is formulated, a contemplative spirit and a deep sense of God are required of those who wish to lead the life of Carmel.

For those who understand how to stay before God, no special activity, no special practical disposition is required. On the contrary, this sense of God, and this thirst to remain in God's presence, do not belong to that category of realities that a Rule or a technique can call into being. Nor can they be developed in any way ascertainable by the sense. They must exist prior to the realization of a contemplative religious life. God is the one who has placed them in the soul's very center and ceaselessly maintains them by means of grace and the Holy Spirit.

This enables us to understand how, although it is not an *institution* in the Western meaning of the term but only a place for the election of a spiritual reality, Carmel has long been able to exist in a free, spontaneous, elementary way and to subsist through the sheer power of its "spirit." This primacy of "spirit," necessary in every religious institute, seems even more necessary in Carmel.

No exterior activity, whatever its form, not even fidelity to the Rule, jealously guarded though this must be, can ever take the place of what ought to be the soul of Carmel, we mean the divine current that reaches the depths of our being and impels Carmelites to return constantly to their center. This search for God, so essential and so secret, leads of itself to simplicity and spiritual poverty. Instinctively the soul seeking God longs to be disencumbered, to be delivered from all things spiritual and material, in order to think of God alone, to be freed from things of the flesh in order to attain to life in the spirit, and to become altogether *spiritual.*

An idea like this necessarily leads to a *spiritual* conception of religious life. In fact, nowhere as much as in Carmel must life and observances be vivified by the spirit. That is why a religious as familiar with the origins of Carmel as John of St. Samson could write in *De la perfection et décadence de la vie religieuse:*

> I say that in the days of these first patriarchs and founders, religious life [at Carmel] was a body strongly and excellently animated by spirit, or rather it was all spirit, and all fervent spirit.

In fact the ideal of Carmel was always, according to the expression of this same author in *Le vrai esprit du Carmel,* "to live in a state of great purity...and to enter into God with all one's strength."

It is obvious that John of St. Samson here refers to the *Book of the Institution of the First Monks,* a text highly representative of the spirit of Carmel and of its oldest and purest mystical traditions. In it we read these lines in which the author seeks to describe the life of the first hermits of Carmel:

> In regard to that life we may distinguish two aims, the one of which we may attain to, with the help of God's grace, by our own efforts and by virtuous living. This is to offer God a heart holy and pure from all actual stain of sin. This aim we achieve when we become perfect, and hidden in Cherith—that is, in that charity of which the Wise One says: *Love covers all offenses.*
>
> The other aim of this life is something that can be bestowed upon us only by God's bounty: namely, to taste in our hearts and experience in our minds, not only after death but even during this mortal life, something of the power of the divine presence, and the bliss of heavenly glory. And this is to *drink from the brook* of the enjoyment of God....[3]

In Carmel, purity of heart is never separated from delight in things divine. The illusion most to be dreaded has always been to aspire to the highest gifts while disdaining or underestimating the necessary purifications. There is another and equally dangerous snare: to try to live a life of high perfection for its own sake and not to aspire to receive the communication of divine life. Carmelite spirituality consists of a supernatural balance that is only possible where there is habitual recourse to the spirit with humility of heart. Although Carmel can see the weakness of its children without astonishment or pessimism, and because it counts on the abundance of divine mercy to remain undisturbed, it has no pity for the slightest shadow that soils the soul. Those who voluntarily harbor some vain attachment in their hearts are not spiritual persons. But of what value is purity without spiritual fruitfulness, or detachment in which there is no love?

In fact, the primacy of God makes it impossible for Carmelites to deviate in their pursuit of their double goal. If they aspire to love with the love of God himself, it is because they are strong in their hope, resolute in their faith, docile in all things to the invitations of the Spirit; it is because they depend on God alone.

Presence to God and Zeal for Souls

No one will be surprised that in such a climate a connatural form of activity will spontaneously come into being; we mean *prayer* understood not so much as an exercise but as *being present to God*. This is altogether objective and interior, silent and sustained, detached and spiritual.

There are no limits to prayer as it is understood in Carmel; just as there are no limits to the quality of interior silence that it realizes and the links it fashions between human beings and their God. According to the measure of the soul's generosity and divine grace, the living God possesses and vivifies this solitude.

The exercise of prayer at Carmel is accompanied by a minimum of material conditions. Prayer involves no rigorously prescribed methods. For its development it requires the liberty and fidelity of a soul constantly visited and vivified by the spirit. The Rule faithfully preserves this conception of life with God. The central obligation there laid down is "to meditate day and night on the Law of the Lord." But the example of Elijah, as well as an inner demand, urges the hermits to realize, both within and outside themselves, a spirit of silence and solitude eminently favorable to prayer, of which the desert is the most perfect expression. The desert calls out to the spirit and the spirit calls out to the desert. Between the spirit of Carmel and the desert there is a living relation. Carmel's prayer is the desert in which the spirit dwells.

But the desert also induces thirst, and prayer slakes the soul's thirst only to create new capacities for the infinite. "Those who drink me will thirst for more" (Sir 24:21). If it is not without meaning that the word of God was heard in a desert, it is equally significant that the possession of the Promised Land was conditioned by an exodus through that same desert. The soul, too, arrives at a meeting with God, in prayer, only at the price of an exodus painful to sense and spirit. But the soul then knows the infinite value of things divine and enjoys that liberty of the children of God that is characteristic of Carmelite spirituality.

This search for God in silence and solitude, this absence of imposed forms of prayer, a conversation that is free and truly heart-to-heart in "the place of the espousals"—this is what the desert means, this is what has characterized Carmel from the beginning. Life of God and desert: these timeless realities are never separated in the Old Testament or in the New. The desert of the soul is the very place of God's communication. "The wilderness and the dry land shall be glad, the desert shall rejoice and blossom" (Is 35:1).

The depths in which the intuitions of the Carmelite soul are rooted may make them seem obscure. They are, nevertheless, astonishingly living and active. Consciously or not, the soul unceasingly returns there, to strive to live them fully and directly.

If no one is more convinced than the Carmelite of the riches and benefits of tradition, it is also true that no one is more faithfully and lovingly attached to it; yet no one else is more fully persuaded that it is necessary to live personally and to experience in direct contact the mystery of God. Tradition may indeed explain and give a love for the divine realities tasted in prayer. But it cannot confer that supreme and incommunicable knowledge that is a fruit of divine wisdom. This comes only to those who open themselves to God in their souls and in their lives. To remain living and active, the revelation of the divine transcendence and mercy ought to be renewed in each one of us.

But as soon as the divine revelation crosses the threshold of our inner dwelling, there is a dawn, and centuries vanish. Those brought back to an absolute beginning watch the flowering of an eternal spring in their own souls. Is not "the verdant one" the meaning of Elijah's name? God himself is there and speaks to the soul. And the soul, making her own the words of the prophet, murmurs:

"The Lord the God of Israel lives, before whom I stand," and "as the Lord lives, and as you yourself live..." (Cf. 1 Kgs 17:1; 2 Kgs 2:6).

The spirit of Carmel is none other than this power and life that spring from the divine word and seek to enter the soul; none other than this divine presence that is waiting to be received and communicated in a reciprocal gift. Today, no more than in the first days, can this word wait for tomorrows in which it will be accomplished.

If the impossible were to take place and the past were suddenly obliterated and tradition no longer existed, and the call of the living God were to sound for the first time in a soul, this call would carry with it the spirit of Carmel in all its freshness, its newness, its eternal richness. Because it is of God and is pure reference to God, this spirit is distinguished by a clarity, a simplicity, and a limpidity that are absolute. It has nothing to do with techniques. It fears more than all else material and spiritual encumbrances, multiplicity of means, devotions, and spiritual exercises. It is God just as God is that it seeks and desires: God, for the mind all mystery, but for the soul light and delicious knowledge.

The spirit of Carmel is a spirit of childhood, of original life, of newness, of immediate proximity to the divine outpouring. It drinks "of the torrent" without a shell; it does not kneel down but stands erect. It is born of God in all its profundity and passes into human beings, renewing and in truth creating them. That is why this spirit is so immediate, so lacking any kind of transition, so without compromise, so bare, with the bare life of the Old Testament; that is why it is so essential. Strengthened by a power that transcends human means and traverses, without ignoring, what is relative, it discovers its goal and goes straight towards it with an all-encompassing exigency of unitive transformation. In short, it advances with a thirst for the absolute that, once felt, can never more be slaked.

Without the least shadow of pessimism, the least disdain for the world, Carmelites are deeply conscious of the infinite distance separating the created from the uncreated, God from God's creatures. Prayer gives them an understanding (better still, permits them to acquire a kind of experience) of the absolute. It is also through prayer that Carmelites, as we read in the second chapter of the *Book of the Institution of the First Monks,* "taste and experience in spirit the power of the divine presence and the sweetness of heavenly glory."

This does not make the spirit of Carmel aloof toward what is created and toward those who live and grow in the earthy and the relative; this experience of God, on the contrary, is the origin of the most active zeal for souls that is characteristic of the action and person of the prophet Elijah. Carmel has never, in fact, separated the apostolic from the contemplative life in its father Elijah "who was afire with zeal for the Lord of hosts" (1 Kgs 19:10, 14), who with fierce energy preserved in the people of Israel belief in the true God, and who has never ceased to serve as a model to the Order that claims him as [spiritual] founder. In 1270–1271, [the prior general] Nicholas the Frenchman...recalled this in these words from his *Ignea Sagitta* [Flaming Arrow]:

> Conscious of their own imperfection, the hermits of Mount Carmel remained long in solitude. But because they desired to be in some way useful to their neighbor, and lest on this point they incur guilt, at times, yet very rarely, they left their hermitage. And as it was with the scythe of contemplation that they harvested in the desert so now in preaching they will scatter the grain on the threshing floor and with open hands they will sow the seed.

So it came about that from the beginning Carmelite prayer has had an apostolic side and overflows with missionary fervor.

Although these spiritual realities are part of the distant epochs of its pre-history, they have come down through the ages and will always be characteristic of Carmel. This inalienable treasure transmitted to us from century to century by the hermits seems to us in its brilliance and marvelous freshness like an ancient jewel discovered in all its beauty in the desert sands.

III. The Rule and Its Spirit

Many centuries have to pass before we possess documents giving evidence of the presence of hermits on Mount Carmel. The first definite text goes back to 1177; it comes to us from the Greek monk John Phocas. Consequently exact information about the kind of life the solitaries led on the mountain of Elijah cannot be obtained before this date.[4]

But by 1209 a hermit community had been established near...Wadi-Ain-Es-Siah (which means "the fountain of Elijah"). There it seems they had settled [some years earlier] and had followed a number of prescriptions belonging to the great monastic tradition. Now they asked Albert, patriarch of Jerusalem, for a Rule which would permit them to lead "the kind of religious observance [they had] chosen," living "a life of allegiance to Jesus Christ," "pure in heart and steadfast in conscience..., unswerving in the service of [their] Master."[5]

In this way a spiritual continuity is established between the *Ermitains dou Carme* [hermits of Carmel] and the *sons of the Prophets.* It also offers proof of the fact that the Rule (which was soon to be that of the Blessed Virgin Mary of Mount Carmel) repudiated nothing of the past. By means of this Rule the hermits living on Carmel were able to live the life of Elijah, their [spiritual] father, in a Christian climate.

The New Testament fulfills the Old. In its turn the Rule of Carmel fulfills the School of the Prophets. The spirituality of Carmel has no difficulty in developing the basic elements drawn from its biblical origins within an evangelic life of perfection. Henceforth it is in the light of Jesus Christ and in dependence on him, characteristics of the Rule from its very first lines, that Carmel's spirituality must be considered.

In fact it is to Christ that the Carmelite turns, offering him prayer and love. And it is following him that the Carmelite intends to walk "pure in heart and steadfast in conscience." Elijah and those who followed him had been in search of all that would lead them to and favor their meeting with God: silence, solitude, desert, sense of the divine absolute, thirst for a direct and ardent contact with God in the heart of prayer. For the Carmelite, all these are a path leading to Jesus Christ, the Son of the Living God.

The Spirituality of the Rule

[Since the *formula vitae* given by Albert] codifies a form of life spontaneously adopted by the hermits and informs us at the same time of the spiritual principles that guided them, a knowledge of this Rule is particularly precious. It not only enables us to discover the spirit of Carmel, but also gives new insights about those whom it binds. John of St. Samson was later to say: "Our primitive Rule is extremely basic and concise; it is more inwardly in regard to the spirit than outwardly in regard to expression." [6]

It is always important to know the spirit in which the special goals of an order are to be sought, as well as the external works for which it was founded. Now the spirit is usually only one of the constituent elements of the order, one characteristic among many others. But when an order has only a spiritual work, and no other end than to promote and sustain spiritual life, then the spirit is everything. The Rule of Carmel makes this clear in its preamble:

> It possesses the austere quality of great spiritual texts, the delicacy of things from above. It seems freed from all accidental detail of space as well as time. Rising above contingencies of matter it does not even stop to discuss questions about the organization of life. It is concerned with what is within. It seeks to waken divine powers slumbering in the contemplative soul. It is an invitation to live rather than a formula of life. [7]

Is it possible to discover the spirit of an interior Rule if one does not possess an interior spirit? From the first, Carmel has insisted on this thirst for solitude and silence, this attraction for the desert as the best place for the divine meeting and for contemplation. The Rule takes this setting on the spiritual plane and makes it interior. The cell becomes the desert where the soul meets its God. Prayer becomes its conversation, its occupation "from morning to night," its "interior life." "Each of you is to stay in your own cell or nearby, pondering the Lord's law day and night and keeping watch at your prayers." [8]

Can the climate of this interior life, of this prayer, be discovered in the Rule? And can the Rule help us to describe the spirituality of Carmel? So sober is the text and so brief that the answer would at first seem to be "no." But considered from within, the text becomes much more revealing.

First of all, this sobriety itself appears eminently characteristic of the spirit that imposed it. It is an immediate introduction to a spirituality freed from the letter and utterly detached. The soul realizes that it must sell all to acquire the hidden treasure, that the kingdom of God alone matters; all else will be given to it over and above.

The sobriety is accompanied by a liberation from every spirit of individualism. Just as "the brother hermits living on Mount Carmel" had recourse to the church in the person of the patriarch of Jerusalem to obtain a Rule (and it will be remembered that when the great reformer [Teresa of Avila] was on her deathbed she gloried only in the fact that she was "a daughter of the church"), so we see even now that the Rule requires that the Divine Office be recited according to the freely embraced "way those holy forefathers of ours laid down, and according to the church's approved custom."

What would [these hermits], fiercely devoted to spiritual liberty and accustomed to the breeze that comes from the desert or the sea, have to do with special forms and complicated methods? Instinctively they cling to what is most simple and ordinary because that is what makes it possible for them to give themselves in peace to "the one thing necessary."

Of course the principle of authority is affirmed, obedience is exacted, as well as silence, work, and the renunciation of all property. But this is to be done in the spirit to which the Gospel has accustomed us. All these are simple means to a single and uniquely necessary end: union with God.

Therefore the Rule is extremely simple and supple, not only because everything in it is ordered and directed to a single end but also because it does not hesitate to make use of all means, according to the gentle and flexible way of the spirit. We read in the Rule:

"You may," "if the Prior and brothers see fit," "where that can be done without difficulty," "unless attending to some other duty," "each one is to receive whatever befits his age and needs," "if it can be done without difficulty," "unless bodily sickness or feebleness, or some other reason, demand a dispensation from the fast, for necessity overrides every law." Nothing cut and dried, nothing narrowly literal, but a simple and truly spiritual means of enabling souls spontaneously to advance in the path of the absolute. This is the spirit of the Gospel: "If you will...."

The Rule is not unaware that a life of union with God rests on the foundation and generous practice of renunciation. But it asks for a renunciation that "without stifling the soul will enable it to be aware of its poverty so that at every instant it will turn toward God." [9] Of course, no progress is possible without effort, and so there is a virile note in every part of the Rule. With Job it repeats that "life on earth is a time of trial" and, [in the words of 2 Timothy], "all who would live devotedly in Christ must undergo persecution." Therefore, "you must use every care to clothe yourselves in God's armor." How could we fail to be reminded, when we see that the Rule lists all the armor recommended by Saint Paul, that it was made for "Crusaders," eager to place themselves at the service of their "Lord" Jesus Christ, Crusaders who were faithful to their ancestors: those great solitaries whose heroic struggles with the flesh and the devil tradition has recorded. But the ascetic side of the Rule is tempered. Effort, renunciation, work, silence appear above all as means of stripping the soul of self, of freeing it so that unhampered it may advance more surely along the paths of divine union.

All that the Rule offers along this line comes straight from the Gospel, whose fragrance it retains. And all this is perfectly integrated with what it has received from its origins. This completes the Rule and adds depth, laying down a path through the desert where the soul can advance without getting lost. "Those who wish to be my disciples must renounce themselves and follow me" [cf. Mk 8:34].

At all times Carmel longed for God. The Rule points out the way. The way does not consist in a series of didactic lessons, or formulas, or techniques, but the study of the living way that is Christ Jesus.

Dependence on Jesus Christ

Henceforth the Carmelite is not to look away from Christ; in dependence on him the Carmelite intends to live. [Carmel's spiritual ancestors] were searching for God and union with God. Then came the Son of God, God himself. Turning towards him, Carmelites did no more than continue along the path that had always been theirs. In virtue of an essential and profound continuity Carmel, which is biblical and remains biblical, becomes evangelical.

In fact, born under the [spirit of the] Old Testament, formed by the divine Word, Carmel awaits its fulfillment. With Elijah and the prophets it watches for "him who is to come"; it can look at nothing else. It finds that, like the prophets, its natural study is to desire the coming of the Savior, to hasten his arrival. Filled with the preparation that abounds in the Sacred Books, Carmel turns toward Christ with the certitude of finding in him all it seeks.

It seeks God as an object of knowledge and love; where then could it better find and embrace him than in his Son who was made flesh and given to us? Carmel awaits the fulfillment of the divine Word. Now Saint John of the Cross tells us that "the Father spoke one Word, which was his Son" [*Sayings,* #100]. Carmel has received as a legacy the awareness of the greatness of God, of the "nothingness" of the creature, and of its divine vocation. How then could it not place all its hope in a Mediator and Savior, all its hope in Christ suffering and dying for us through love?

Nevertheless, considered relatively, Christ's role in the Rule is lightly stressed. Here we are in the presence of one of Carmel's mysteries. It is not easy to grasp: a hidden, half-formulated spiritual reality that is at the same time truly central and profoundly operative.

Beyond any doubt there are other schools of spirituality in which Christ's role is more prominent. He is the model, the exemplar, and his life must be imitated. The spirituality of a contemplative order could never be like that. If it is a question of always looking at Christ, it is also and even more a question of uniting oneself to him and living by him. Christ who is the way toward the Father, the author and finisher of our faith, becomes by this fact, the *milieu* in which contemplation develops, the *path* it uses. So it would seem the [focus of] Carmel's Rule is on Christ and that Carmelite prayer develops in the depths of the life Christ communicates to the soul.

Certainly Carmel is not unmindful of the need of some kind of a method, but it seems that those who had asked for the Rule had already made some progress in the spiritual life. This is because they had been leading for a long time a solitary, interior, and mortified life, and they possessed "a pure heart and steadfast conscience." Therefore the Rule is more interested in highlighting what must be characteristic of contemplative life: perpetual prayer to which the hermits must dedicate themselves—"these continual vigils of prayer must make [religious] the Lord's intimate friends, and love becomes a state of soul." [10]

The Rule does not define the nature of the contemplation toward which it is oriented, but it is easy to discover it in the *Book of the Institution of the First Monks*. This document was long held in the same reverence as the primitive Rule and allows us to understand that this perpetual prayer must make it possible for Carmelites "in some way to taste in their hearts and to experience in their souls the strength of the divine presence and the sweetness of heavenly glory: in other words to drink from the torrent of divine pleasure."

Clearly this is a reference to a mystical experience of God. This is, in fact, the end toward which the Order is oriented. Of course not all reach the goal. But at least Christ is for all the path that leads to the goal. And all ought to live "a life of allegiance to Jesus Christ," all ought "to remain in their cells...meditating on the Law of the Lord day and night and keeping watch at prayer."

Brothers and Sisters of Our Lady

Directed to Christ and oriented to him, Carmel is also directed to Mary and oriented to her. "Completely Marian," *Totus marianus est,* Carmelite authors like to repeat throughout the centuries, and of all their titles none is dearer to the sons [and daughters] of Elijah than that of Brothers [and Sisters] of our Lady.

It is historically certain that the first hermits who retired to Mount Carmel...made their center a chapel consecrated to our Lady, and from the time of...the first Prior General, the Carmelites were called *Brothers of our Lady of Mount Carmel.* So devotion to our

Lady is seen to be one of their distinctive signs. "Despite its histori-cal inexactitudes the *Book of the Institution of the First Monks* shows that the Order is dominated by the two great figures which repre-sent, on different levels, its ideal: Elijah and our Lady." [11]

No need to follow the example of medieval Carmelite au-thors, in particular [Arnold] Bostius [1445–1499], and multiply the subtle and often forced resemblances between Elijah and our Lady. The origin of these resemblances is to be found in a mystical inter-pretation of the scene in the first book of Kings where on the heights of Carmel, at the prophet's prayer, a little cloud, about as big as the palm of one's hand, rises out of the sea, melts into rain and fructifies the parched land: this is [seen as] the image of the Virgin who was to give the Savior to humanity (1 Kgs 18:44). Nor is it necessary to do what [John] Baconthorpe [d. 1348] did about 1330 and seek to establish close parallels between the life led by the Carmelite and the life of our Lady. "We have chosen a Rule," he said, "in which many points are similar to the life led by the Blessed Virgin Mary."

If this is so, why does this Rule never once mention our Lady's name? Nor is the name of Elijah found in its pages (in fact no ref-erence is made to the fountain *of Elijah* in the primitive texts). Nev-ertheless it is certain, as the Order's many authors and documents repeat, that Carmel belongs to Elijah and to our Lady. "Marianus et Elianus Ordo Carmeli" [the Marian and Elijan Order of Carmel] is the way it is expressed in the *Mirror of the Carmelites,* or the *History of the Order of Elijah of the Brothers of the Blessed Virgin Mary of Mount Carmel.*

At Carmel what is true of our Lord is also true of our Lady. Contemplative life advances by assimilation and union, much more than by images, examples, and models. Preserving all due propor-tion, what we have said of Christ we repeat about Mary. If Carmelites do not strive to imitate Mary's life [in its historical de-tails], they do find themselves quite naturally in deep harmony with her soul, and it is in this sense that they may be said to lead a "Mary-form" life.

Our Lady is for Carmelites not only the Mother of Christ and their own mother. She also represents and expresses the soul's es-sential attitude before God. Mary not only sums up the whole Old

Testament, she represents all humanity. She is its soul athirst for
God, longing for God, hoping for God. All her strength and all her
faculties are turned toward God so that she may receive and fully
live by him. Our Lady is also the place of the divine response, of
the divine coming. In her, humanity becomes conscious of God's
desire and fully efficacious will to give himself to us. Mary is the
place of this meeting; better still, she is the temple in which is con-
summated God's espousals with humanity, the hidden sanctuary in
which the Spouse is united with the bride, the desert that flowers at
the breath of God.

Our Lady is pure reference to God and to the life of God in
the sense in which Elisha said to Elijah: "As the Lord lives and as
your soul lives." From the moment of her immaculate conception
Mary's soul had no other life than God, no other end than to know
God and to love God purely and without any admixture and to allow God to accomplish in her his designs of love. Carmel finds in
Mary the fullness of the spirit that is its own: her beauty is without
spot, her purity is absolute. As Isaiah says: "The beauty of Carmel
will be given you" (35:2). Reciprocally, Mary's soul is connected
with Carmel. She is a daughter of David according to the flesh, the
daughter of the prophets and the daughter of Elijah according to
the spirit.

In biblical times souls sought to make the perfect response
that Mary was to give to the Word of God which "she pondered in
her heart" (Lk 2:19) and on which she "meditated day and night."
They longed for the ardent zeal with which she was aflame under
the action of the Spirit of God. But her virginal maternity made this
predestined daughter of Carmel a queen and raised her to a place
of sovereignty among her brothers and sisters. For this reason,
Carmel will live Mary and will breathe Mary with a movement as
natural and spontaneous as it is willed and conscious. To advance
along this path Carmelites have but to intensify their Marian attitude of virginal simplicity and pure reference to God. In Carmel
God is the objective, but the soul will become more and more Mary.

So the reason why the Rule does not mention our Lady is
clear. Carmel seeks to gaze upon God and love God with mind and
heart. What Mary represents is the soul itself. As the soul is united
to Christ, so Carmel is hidden in Mary. For Carmel, Mary is, beyond

any doubt, the infinitely admirable and lovable Mother, the all-merciful Mother, but deeper than this, she is the one who was chosen and formed by God to be the Mother of the Savior; she is the purest, highest, and most perfect expression of the soul that is open to the divine action and lives in Mary's light and in Mary's love. She is, *par excellence,* the contemplative soul.

This mystic and filial intuition was to be confirmed in the centuries that were to come. In a critical hour, [according to tradition] our Lady herself answered the trusting, insistent prayer of Saint Simon Stock. She appeared to him, holding in her hand the scapular of the Order, and said: "This is the privilege that I give you and all Carmel's children. Whoever dies clothed with this habit will be saved." [12] In this way she extended, in visible fashion, her special protection over the Order that has always called itself her own.

Mary was to intervene in the lives of Carmel's saints. Saint Albert of Sicily, Saint Andrew Corsini, Saint Peter-Thomas, Saint Teresa, Saint John of the Cross, and in our own days Saint Thérèse of the Child Jesus were favored with our Lady's visible protection. It seems as if in Carmel there can be no great servant of God who has not been sustained and guided by Mary.

Similarly, Carmel's authors multiply works that tighten the already close bonds between Carmel and our Lady. The Order was founded for the veneration of the Blessed Virgin. The Rule, [claims John Baconthorpe in his *Treatise on the Rule*], was formulated in connection with her life and virtues. In one sense, the objectivity and [historical] value of these connections matter little. It is certain that between the time of the Rule and the Reform, "the idea of our Lady taken as model greatly gained in precision...and it becomes clear that Carmel was established for her honor." Was it not normal, and at the same time the manifestation of an altogether filial spirit, for Carmel to give the Blessed Virgin Mary honor that expressed something of her own intimate fervor?

> The first hermits of Carmel considered Carmelite life as an existence dedicated equally to the service of the Lord God and of his Mother, the Virgin Mary. Better than all the legends, this expression permits us to understand the flowering of Marian

piety at Carmel and the true meaning of later official texts which affirmed that the Order of Carmel is dedicated from its beginning to the honor of our Lady.[13]

Apostolic Contemplation

The Rule that keeps Carmelite spirituality along interior and contemplative lines and gives it its evangelical and Marian character equally confirms the apostolic orientation that it received from the patriarch Elijah himself. If he pronounced the sentence on which the contemplative spirit is based, "the Lord lives before whom I stand," he also proclaimed, "I am consumed with zeal for the Lord of hosts."

Within limits suitable to the Order, the Rule faithfully maintains this apostolic note in the spirituality of Carmel. The only reason Carmelites are allowed to interrupt their "meditation on the Law of the Lord," and leave for a time the silence and recollected solitude of their cells, is for the salvation of souls. This orientation is clearly marked in the Rule and explains why [Carmelite friars] can be classified among the mendicant orders that by principle are devoted to the care of souls. It is also classified among the orders that are called *mixed* because they are directed to both contemplation and action.

Therefore whatever be the dangers of "activism" and the attractions of the apostolate, the [Carmelite] spirituality of the apostolate will never be that of an exclusively contemplative order. When the popes ask the Carmelite friars to give missions, to preach, to undertake good works, the invitation will never be refused on the grounds that the Carmelite's vocation is purely contemplative.

On the other hand, how many are the appeals made to the Order by its great spiritual leaders, how many the efforts made by its superiors to prevent Carmel from being gradually transformed into an [exclusively] active order. Contemplation is the heart of Carmel, its reason, its distinguishing mark, its protection. If there must be some interruption "even though it be necessary and for a short space of time," as soon as their work is done Carmelites must quickly return to the primary and direct object of their vocation.

In the *Ignea Sagitta* [Flaming Arrow], Nicholas the Frenchman recalls with vigor and sorrow the Order's contemplative traditions that he believed to be endangered. Adding example to words, he withdrew to a hermitage. In his turn, Ralph de Fryston, who succeeded him, did exactly the same thing. The general chapter of Montpellier (1287) took various measures to maintain in the Order "the citadel of contemplation." Retreat and solitude were recommended in every Constitution. That is why *deserts* will later appear, for without them Carmel lacks one of its essential elements. The neighbor's needs may well draw Carmelites to the apostolate, but something still stronger must constantly draw them back to their solitude; because in the last analysis it is there, in their heart-to-heart union with God, that they will produce the true fruits of the apostolate, because the fruitfulness of their life is measured by the purity of their love for God.

This *better part*, which in Carmel is contemplation, was to be constantly threatened until Saint Teresa's reform. The Order was introduced into the West in the thirteenth century. It became more and more involved in the intellectual and social life of its age and like most religious orders it was subjected to influences that brought about its decline. In the case of Carmel, this decline came from the gradual abandonment of contemplative life, the giving up of what John Soreth calls "continual, uninterrupted persevering prayer," or "that union with God which is not only habitual but actual" which Father Rubeo [i.e., the prior general John Rossi] of Ravenna recommended on the eve of the Teresian reform.

Had Carmel remained truly faithful to this central precept of prayer, recollection, and a life of union with God—yet at the same time without giving up its apostolate—no Teresian reform might have been necessary. Perhaps there is no better way than this of showing how essential to Carmelite spirituality is this priority of contemplation [as the source of all apostolic] action that alone makes possible the preservation intact of its true ideal. For its restoration Saint Teresa "will live alone with the Alone," and will establish her daughters in strict enclosure; and Saint John of the Cross, the great doctor of life hidden with God, will sacrifice his life. Nothing less than the genius, the efforts, the sufferings of these two great saints were needed so that the pure spirit of its origins could flourish once again in the Order of the blessed Virgin Mary of Mount Carmel.[14]

IV. Masters and Models

Enriched by its long past and bearing its precious heritage, Carmel reached the period of its reform. To consider this reform apart from the whole tradition and to fail to link the reformers, Saint Teresa and Saint John of the Cross, to their own spiritual family, would be to give an incomplete idea of Carmelite spirituality and an inaccurate picture of the reform itself.

The power of their genius, made fruitful by their holiness, cannot be denied, and the light and penetration they have given Carmel are obvious. Raised up by God at a moment both critical and propitious, they brought Carmel back to life, but they did not give life to Carmel. Before their reform Carmel existed, and one of its two chief branches owes nothing to these two very pure lights, and has continued to flourish.

Because of their nearness to us, Saint Teresa and Saint John of the Cross seem alone to represent Carmel and we cannot imagine Carmel without them. Certainly it is not for a [Discalced] Carmelite to underestimate their role and their glory; to do so would be to strike at his [spiritual] father and mother. But how could we lessen their glory by situating them in this long and glorious line of spiritual men and women who throughout the centuries have formed Carmel? Was this not what Saint Teresa herself felt and wanted when she wrote in the *Way of Perfection:* "The style of life we aim to follow is not just that of nuns but of hermits" (13, 6). "Let us remember our holy fathers of the past, those hermits whose lives we aim to imitate" (11, 4).

Saints are like that! Their way of remaining faithful to tradition or of returning to it is so richly alive, so full of the spirit of God that they create something new: *nova et vetera* [new and old]. Without changing any of the features they give the beloved face a new youthfulness: "Send forth your spirit and they shall be created and you shall renew the face of the earth" [cf. Ps 104:30].

The influence of Saint Teresa on Carmel's spirituality differs greatly from that of Saint John of the Cross because of differences in the personality and temperament of the two reformers and because of the different roles they were called upon to play. Yet they complement one another perfectly.

SAINT TERESA

That Saint Teresa was first and foremost a contemplative cannot be denied. It is in fact in the domain of prayer and mystical life that she deepened and enriched Carmelite spirituality. But her personality and her role went further than this, because it was with her whole being that she gave herself to a life of union with God. Stripping herself of all things without repudiating any of them, it is the totality of her aspirations, her heart, her strength, and her life that she willed to make subject to God. So it is not only the understanding of religious life but also of the spiritual life that was enriched and renewed, first in Saint Teresa herself, and then in the Carmel of which she was the mother and the reformer.

Saint Teresa's realism is so deep and so authentic that even unconsciously she strove to make an organic whole and a living unity of the different parts of her existence. Prayer is the source of the life and movement of this organic whole; it is the principle of unitive transformation. But it attains its end only when it is able to orient all the different parts of religious life toward the same end, and to give the same directive idea to every aspect of daily life and even to the most humble forms of activity.

Saint Teresa's contributions to Carmelite spirituality are not to be found merely in her writings (revealing though these may be), for they were never anything more than occasional compositions in which were mirrored God's action in her soul or in her life. Her contributions are to be discovered and examined first in her work as a reformer because, in a certain sense, she modeled Carmel after her own image—not that she pointed her ideal in a new direction, but that she strongly impressed it with her genius. So it is in the Constitutions and in the form of religious life that she asked her daughters to follow, no less than in her writings, that we must look for the elements that henceforth were to characterize Carmel's spirituality.

Double and single movements of love
↑ to God
↓
`one theological virtue of charity`

36 Brothers & Sisters. *Paul-Marie of the Cross, OCD*

In this, Saint Teresa's influence is sharply distinguished from that of Saint John of the Cross. There can be no doubt, as we shall see, that he was, from the first instant, won to the cause of reform. Moreover, he remained at Carmel only on condition that the reform be carried out. But even though he worked heroically for its success, he is preeminent because it was in this setting that he achieved perfect spiritual liberty, and complete mystical development. Saint Teresa first reconstructed the Carmelite dwelling, then reestablished its foundations and created therein a climate eminently favorable for true spiritual life; Saint John of the Cross, having come to the end of the most amazing of journeys to the realm of mystical union, then laid down its principles, traced its routes, and described all its riches.

Like the commandment bequeathed to us by our Lord, Carmel is wholly concentrated on a double and single movement of love. Double, because it is directed to God and to our brothers and sisters. Single, because the one theological virtue of charity informs the two movements, the two tempos of Carmelite spirituality that give it its vital rhythm and are, as it were, its heartbeat and its breath. Even before she thought of this rhythm, Teresa had lived it intensely. Therefore this double movement marks her reform because her life was lived according to the spirit of Carmel; that is to say, she gave the preponderant place, the "better part," to contemplation.

She was a realist, so she understood that the whole life of Carmel had to be reconsidered as a function of contemplative life. Strict enclosure, silence, work in solitude must be [established] so that union with God could develop in most favorable surroundings. Under an original yet basically traditional form, Carmel was to live again the life and spirit of its origins, thanks to Saint Teresa. The best proof of this is given us by the response the Carmelites themselves made to the reform. If Saint John of the Cross and the first discalced were won over to the reform, it is because they discovered in it what we have attempted to analyze: this primitive spirit, this original soil, without which nothing would flower, without which Carmel would cease to be.

Only the analysis of the ensemble of the works of Saint Teresa, of her spiritual counsels, of her mystical experiences—all of which help to restore true contemplative life, the true life of union with God—can reveal her true role.

It cannot be denied that the Saint has her own way of looking at contemplative life. Her experience of this life, on the mystical plane, is unique. But this way and this experience, however original they may be, are situated well within the boundaries of Carmelite spirituality. And the form of life that she [established] appears, in the light of experience, to be the best adapted to the requirements and aspirations of contemplative souls.

A woman's way of thinking about union with God cannot be exactly the same as that of religious men. Although the ideal is the same for all, it must be approached differently and attained by different paths. Saint Teresa understood this perfectly. Beginning with a conviction and a deep contemplative and mystical experience, she considered each detail of religious life not only as a function of the sought-for goal but also in terms of concrete feminine nature.

A highly developed sense of moderation, coupled with a penetrating psychology, in short, a profound wisdom mark the Constitutions to which she gave a realistic foundation. Because of her unflagging efforts, the idea of contemplative life ceased to be abstract and vague. It found its way into and became an integral part of the tiniest acts of life. An intimate bond united prayer and life, morality and mysticism, exterior conduct and union with God. Between a life of highest mysticism and the gift of self, between the soul's need to love and the most lowly forms of fraternal charity, Teresa created links, established relations, forged tight bonds.

In contemplative and religious life as she understood and organized it, an organic unity was realized, not by outer pressure but by an inner principle both gentle and strong: this principle was love. The soul that contemplates must long to give itself to the one whom it loves. It must long to be one with God and to serve God.

This organic unity was realized according to the norms of a higher wisdom. As one of her recent biographers has correctly observed:

> Teresa was able to resolve with classic good sense, let us say catholic good sense, two delicate problems: that of the

requirements of human nature and union with God; that of the relation between the personal development of the mystical life and the framework in which common religious life is inserted. If the asceticism that she practiced, and on whose necessity she insisted, was always intransigent, it was also always reasonable. The humble realities of life here below are the foundation on which one must build in order that the spirit may ascend to God. Progress is conditioned by these foundations, just as the life of the tree is determined by its roots; to neglect the first, to destroy or to paralyze the second, would be fatal.[15]

To Saint Teresa, Carmel owes its *élan* and its psychology. Carmelite psychology was always realistic. Under the reformer's influence it became more so. In fact, her prudence and supernatural wisdom made her require that contemplative life—and mystical experience when this is added—be made more and more dependent on [Christian doctrine], the sacraments, obedience to the church and to superiors, the practice of virtues, fidelity to the Rule. Only in this way can sentimentalism, illuminism, and quietism in any form whatsoever be avoided.

Better than anyone else did she understand and highlight what is basic in the spiritual life: the need to make everything rest on the renunciation of self-will, generosity carried to the point of perfection in carrying out the duties of one's state of life, charity to one's brothers and sisters, bearing with one's neighbor. It is virtues like these that, in their realism, support the whole spiritual edifice and assure its unity. There can be no division in being, no dichotomy between life that is purely human and life-made-divine.

A mystical life that insists on purest realism ensures the supreme unity of its being. This organic unity—with all the intercommunication of all its inner elements whose life is derived from a higher principle—this is one of the most precious legacies that Carmelite spirituality owes to Saint Teresa.

It is essentially by means of prayer that Saint Teresa believes this higher principle will reign in the soul and will provide this organic unity. Everyone knows that Saint Teresa was the great teacher of prayer. On this capital point her contribution is as traditional as it is original.

It is traditional because, like all the spiritual men and women who preceded her, Saint Teresa wanted to orient contemplatives toward the summit of union with God. This result and this grace she thought they would find in prayer, because in prayer God and the soul, although working on different planes, unite their efforts. She was also traditional in teaching (on this point she resembled her predecessors) that the contemplative ideal of transforming union is not *extraordinary*. She believed that it was the integral fullness of spiritual life. So she aspired to it, though with humility, because infused contemplation always remains an absolutely gratuitous divine gift.

At the same time, Saint Teresa showed her originality in not being satisfied with assigning this goal to the contemplative life; she pointed out the paths that lead to this goal. Her teaching was marked by a wealth of experience and a psychological depth that have not yet been equaled, as well as by a singularly noble and profound conception of a life of union with God. "The important thing" in prayer "is not to think much but to love much" [*Castle*, 4, 1, 7]. And for Teresa:

> To love is to surrender one's self without reserve. This means to surrender one's will in such a way to the divine will, however crucifying it may be, that one finds joy in suffering when this is pleasing to the Beloved; and this intense love is a call for God's presence. The soul enraptured by God tends spontaneously to possess God. The ideal of perfect self-donation corresponds quite naturally in her doctrine with the desire for mystical union. God must be generous to the generous soul.... The soul's total gift calls for the total gift of God.[16]

In prayer, as Teresa experienced it and as she taught it to her daughters, Christ's position is dominant. This is one of the original points of her spirituality. Admittedly before her time Christ's presence was implicit and active in every part of Carmel's spiritual life, but his role was not sharply defined. Saint Teresa brought him to the fore as never before. "This method of keeping Christ present with us is beneficial in all stages and is a very safe means of advancing in the first degree of prayer, of reaching in a short time the second degree, and of walking secure against the dangers the devil can set up in the last degrees" (*Life*, 12, 3). No statement could be clearer.

Because Teresa gave so important a place to Christ in prayer, it is highly important to understand what he meant to her. No less important is it to trace her spiritual evolution on this point.

Christ was everything to Teresa. This is undeniable. "Speak with him as with a father, or a brother, or a lord, or as with a spouse" (*Way*, 28, 3). She cherished him with the tenderness of a mother, the respect of a daughter, the love of a spouse. But in this love there "is never anything that is not spiritual" (*Castle*, 5, 4, 3). In fact "the spiritual joys the Lord gives when compared to the delights married people must experience are a thousand leagues distant," since "it is all a matter of love united with love" (*Castle*, 5, 4, 3).

If Christ is able to raise Teresa above every sensible affection, while "keeping alive her powers of loving, it is because she realizes that he is the eternal, the transcendent; it is because he is the absolute, the infinite; it is because he is God." [17] There can be no doubt that even in God, Teresa cannot get along without a heart that loves. But Teresa never forgets that the heart that Christ gives her to love in his humanity is a divine Heart. If some souls find that the humanity of Christ is for them an obstacle, it is because they do not think of him as they should.

> This Lord of ours is the one through whom all blessings come to us.... Blessed are they who truly love him and always keep him at their side! Let us consider the glorious St. Paul: it doesn't seem that any other name fell from his lips than that of Jesus, as coming from the one who kept the Lord close to his heart. Once I had come to understand this truth, I carefully considered the lives of some of the saints, the great contemplatives, and found that they hadn't taken any other path: St. Francis demonstrates this through the stigmata; St. Anthony of Padua, with the Infant; St. Bernard found his delight in the humanity; St. Catherine of Siena—and many others.... (*Life*, 22, 7)

So Teresa's decision was made. On this road there are so many advantages of love and faith, that she offered her daughters the humanity of Jesus as the path *par excellence* and the ordinary way for all (see *Castle*, 6, 7, 1ff.).

Yet the evolution of Christ's role in the Saint's prayer is no less revealing than the position he holds. At the beginning Teresa kept Christ before her eyes, but gradually she began to meditate on the mystery of his Person. Soon she saw in him most of all a guide and a companion; then Jesus Christ became for her the way, the path to the Father, the light in which we see him. Teresa united herself to God by the Word Incarnate. Finally, with Christ's help, Teresa was led to the Blessed Trinity whose importance never ceased to increase in her interior life.

> From this we must not conclude that Jesus Christ was relegated to a secondary place but that he no longer was seen in the same perspective. He continues to be Man who, being God, reveals God to all who will listen to him and contemplate him...but he is above all the Incarnate Word with whom the soul must be united in order to make some return through him to the Father in the unity of the Holy Spirit.[18]

This was the way Christ led Teresa to the Triune God. He taught her to be aware of God as her last end, absolute Omnipotence, the answer to the call of her whole soul. He led her to the heart of the mystery that is the origin and goal of all mystical life. It is true that Christ's role, indispensable though he be, since "no one comes to the Father" except through him (Jn 14 6), is apparently less visible in certain mystics who seem lost in the divine darkness; but in Saint Teresa's teaching he shines with a brilliant light from which Carmelite spirituality will always benefit.

> The Saint's first intention was merely to found a monastery where she and those who wished to follow her could, with the help of a more strict enclosure and a more austere life, keep the promises they had made to the Lord according to the vocation of their Order. Later, realizing the vast needs of the church, and desiring in her great charity to assist those who were fighting for her, she went still further, as far as this was possible.[19]

In strengthening the bonds that united her with Jesus Christ and his church, Teresa acted according to the most orthodox mysticism. This was also according to Carmelite spirituality. On this

point, as well as on the two preceding questions, no one can fail to
see the richness and the originality of her contribution.

It is, in fact, with Jesus Christ that Saint Teresa begins her
deep understanding of the reality of the church. Of course her sub-
mission to the church had always been completely loyal and even
fervently joyous—and remained so until the end. Yet there is more
than this in her dying cry: "I am a daughter of the church." She was
referring not only to the visible church, the traditional church
rooted deep in her Spanish soul, this church from whom, without
ignoring its human aspects and its weaknesses, she never ceased to
ask for a rule of faith, a rule of life and light for the guidance of her
soul. To her, the church was Christ, above all else.

This enlightened and universal view of the church and the
absolute confidence she pledged to it are possible only because of
her mystical union with Christ. To Teresa, the church is not only
an intensely vital reality, it is also an institution established on dog-
matic foundations that are very sure and very rich. It is the church
that asks of us in Christ's name not [merely] a contemplative and
unitive love but an active love. To Teresa the church means Christ
and souls, that is to say, now and always she considered the mystery
of Christ from the apostolic point of view. The second commandment is like the first [cf. Mt 22:39] and flows from it.

It follows that divine love, in Teresa's eyes, never ceases to
grow but radiates in ever widening concentric circles, just as waves
move outward from a center. Fraternal and supernatural charity is
directed first to all those who live in the monastery, then with constantly renewed fervor and strength it is transformed into a love for
souls, for all souls, that is to say, for the whole church. "A soul who
aspires to become the spouse of God himself...cannot allow itself a
sluggard's rest. The redemptive God gives his life and self-giving
love to the soul who gives herself to him" (cf. *Castle*, 5, 4, 10). Less
than a century later a voice from "beyond the Pyrenees" answered
like an echo: "This is no time to sleep."

Christ is always "the center of this apostolate," and Teresa
never forgets that this [apostolate] must be *contemplative* above all
else. So she sees that this is first the practice of virtue, fidelity to the
Rule, renunciation and the cross. Then (and this is its real meaning) she sees that the apostolate is a form of prayer, that is to say, it

is love in action. "The more [persons] advance in this kind of prayer and the gifts of our Lord the more attention they pay to the needs of their neighbor, especially to the needs of their neighbors' souls" (*Meditations on the Song of Songs,* 7, 8).

Just like her [spiritual] daughter Saint Thérèse of the Child Jesus, the first Teresa burned with the desire to be a doctor, a missionary, an apostle; she longed to make God's name known and his kingdom come in every part of the world. A zeal much like that of her father Elijah entered her prayer and made it a prayer of fire. Her writings are in their own way another form of this zeal, and they show us that she was constantly "filled with the ardent desire of being useful to souls." She was "grief-stricken over the loss of so many souls" (*Foundations,* 1, 7). She "would have given a thousand lives to save one soul" (*Way,* 1, 3). She spent her time "occupied in prayer for those who are the defenders of the church and for preachers and for [theologians]" (*Way,* 1, 3). She wrote: "I tried to please the Lord with my poor prayers and always endeavored that the Sisters would do the same and dedicate themselves to the good of souls and the increase of his church.... And these were the things with which my great desires were taken up" (see *Foundations,* 1, 6ff.).

But this active and apostolic woman never failed to give to her action and her apostolic work the seal of Carmelite spirituality, which is primarily contemplative. She said that at the beginning of the contemplative life we ought to "consider that there is nothing on earth but God and oneself" (*Life,* 13, 9). Otherwise the soul would "lose" itself in the world. When it is a little more advanced—its faculties now at rest—God will ripen the fruits of its garden so that it can draw strength from them. This is what God wants. However, he does not want the soul to distribute the fruits of its garden before it has first been strengthened by them. Otherwise the "soul will only learn to taste them...and will eventually die of hunger."

It is...when the soul has attained to union, and God has taken possession of the very depths of the soul, that good works are required: "Once the soul has reached this point, it no longer offers God simple desires; his majesty gives it the strength to carry them out." [20]

Therefore to become an apostle, the soul must love, love without any reserve, and give itself totally to God. Once again, Teresa has rediscovered and completely renewed the spirit of her Order, which has two purposes, one dependent on the other: contemplation that unites the soul with God and reveals the infinite value of souls, then overflows in the apostolate.

These are the contributions that Saint Teresa made to Carmelite spirituality: she re-thought and reformed the whole contemplative life in terms of the true and pure Carmelite ideal; she renewed and deepened the life of prayer founded in Christ, experiencing and describing all its stages as far as the highest states of pure mysticism; she held broad and safe views of the church and of Carmel's apostolate. She poured out these riches in a climate marked by freedom, fervor, and balance, in an atmosphere of expansive and undisturbed joy.

So we see why she continues to be the most radiant figure of Carmel and how, like the spouse of the Canticle, she continues to attract souls to Christ: "Draw me: we will run after thee" (Song 1:3).

SAINT JOHN OF THE CROSS

Carmelite spirituality owes just as much to Saint John of the Cross as it does to Saint Teresa. At first sight the audience and the influence of the Mystical Doctor seem destined to remain very restricted. Did he not address himself to:

> ...some of the persons of our holy order of the primitive observance of Mount Carmel, both friars and nuns, whom God favors by putting on the path leading up this mount [of Carmel].... Because they are already detached to a great extent from the temporal things of this world, they will more easily grasp this doctrine on nakedness of spirit. (*Ascent*, Prologue, 9)

Nevertheless experience proves that the saint's influence was not limited and that it increased and went far beyond the walls of Carmel. No doubt this is to be explained by the fact that Saint John of the Cross pursued a single objective with a clarity of vision that was equaled only by the rigor of his teaching and the heroic fixity of a will focused on the absolute. What did he actually ask? Nothing else than to go on as far as divine union in transforming love. And what does he teach? The spiritual attitude necessary for one who would arrive promptly at the summit of the Mount of Perfection. Now "whatever may be the mountain in our life, and whatever form it may take, there is a straight path leading to the summit, and it is this way that he wishes to point out to souls." [21]

Therefore a soul who is resolved to advance towards sanctity, and feels inwardly attracted to Saint John's abrupt and direct method, will find precious help in this sure and experienced guide. Did he not, like his Master, begin *to do* before he began *to teach*?

The Mystical Doctor considers mystical life under its essential and complementary aspects. First, he discusses the work of detachment in a soul advancing toward God; then he examines God's direct action on a soul who submits passively to this divine action. He then sings of the joys and splendors of divine union. In other words, his work embraces the whole question of the transformation of our being and our way of acting under the influence of the Spirit of God.

Heroically faithful to the spirit of the primitive Rule that Saint Teresa, in reforming the Order, made it possible for him to live, and focusing on its essential precept (union with God in uninterrupted prayer), Saint John of the Cross has given us a work that is unique because of the richness of his experience (as much psychological as mystical) and the holiness of his life. He goes beyond pure speculation because he wants, lovingly, tenderly, and warmly, to persuade souls to journey along the path to divine union and to show them its treasures. To do this he makes use of a very rare poetic gift that enables him sweetly to communicate to souls the lights he has received and the living flame of his love for God.

Which Path Leads to the Summit of the Mount of Perfection?

With the whole tradition of Carmel to support him, John of the Cross unhesitatingly answers, "the path of the Bible and the Gospel, that is to say, the path that is Christ." At Carmel, the soul always draws strength from the divine Word. Of course this means both the Old and New Testaments, for Carmel's roots are fixed deep in Scripture. John of the Cross kept the Bible and two or three other books of piety in his cell. He never ceased to read and meditate the Bible. In it he not only searched for a knowledge of revelation, but he also believed that he could find in its pages the laws that always govern the dealings of the Holy Spirit with souls.

Did he think that beyond the literal meaning one ought to look for a deep mystical and spiritual meaning? Of course, it is the Spirit alone who possesses the secret of this mystical meaning, and it has been promised infallibly only to the church, but the Spirit grants it also to those who humbly follow the guidance of the church in their search. John is skilled in this exegesis and his interpretations are those of a master. He believes that Scripture is the rule and measure of progress in the interior life and that it enlarges one's own experience, containing as it does innumerable examples from the past.[22]

But God's word means above all the Gospels. In truth, "in many and various ways God spoke of old to our ancestors by the prophets, but in these last days he has spoken to us by a Son" (Heb 1:1–2). And the mystical doctor has declared that "the Father spoke one Word, which was his Son" (*Sayings*, #100). And on another occasion he said: "In giving us his Son, his only Word (for he possesses no other), [God] spoke everything to us at once.... Fasten your eyes on him alone because in him [God has] spoken and revealed all" (*Ascent*, 2, 22, 3–5; see also *Ascent*, 2, 7, 5–12).

As a matter of fact Saint John's teaching, like his life, was obviously based on the Gospels. He has placed himself in Christ's heart and in the heart of Christ's teaching. It is true that his speculative study of the spiritual life does not seem [at first glance] to be Christocentric. Nevertheless in it he forcefully affirms that no union with God is possible except in Christ (ibid.), and this is true both of faith (which is adhesion to God in Christ) and of life. To reach God we must make Christ our model. Saint John wants us always to desire to act like Christ. "Of what use is this life if it does not give us the opportunity of acting like Christ?" Christ crucified is the synthesis of his whole doctrine. "Let Christ crucified be enough for you, and with him suffer and take your rest" (*Sayings*, #92).

When he had reached the goal of mystical life he declared that knowledge of Christ's mysteries is the highest wisdom possible in this life: "And having ascended above all things, in solitude from all things, [the soul] profits by no other than the Word, the Bridegroom, who helps her to ascend further" (*Canticle*, 35, 6).

"Let the soul long to enter into the darkness of the Cross, which is the way of life." And perfection in the spiritual life will mean nothing else than an immense love of extreme poverty and suffering for the sake of the Beloved: "Love consists not in feeling great things but in having great detachment and in suffering for the Beloved" (*Sayings*, #115), that is to say, "for this great God of ours, crucified and humbled" (*Letters*, #25).

The Shepherd who "spread his arms, ...his heart an open wound with love" (*Poems*, #7, 5) dominates the life of Saint John of the Cross.

If the Mystical Doctor carries, as he does, the image of the Crucified in his heart, it is also on the Crucified that he bases his whole doctrine. "Those who wish to come after me, must deny themselves and take up their cross and follow me" [Mk 8:34]. It is truly the Gospel teaching that is the foundation of the saint's teaching.

To imitate Christ, "renounce and remain empty of any sensory satisfaction that is not purely for the honor and glory of God," and "do this out of love for Jesus Christ" (*Ascent*, 1, 13, 4). Renunciation and love, is this not a complete description of Christ? It is also a complete description of Saint John of the Cross.

Therefore it is within this frame of reference that we must consider his doctrine: detachment in all things through absolute attachment to Christ. Renunciation is the obverse of love. "To come to possess all, desire the possession of nothing" (*Ascent*, 1, 13, 11). "For Christ, desire to enter into complete nakedness, emptiness, and poverty in everything in the world" (*Ascent*, 1, 13, 6). Saint John of the Cross was to speak of this renunciation as no one else had ever done before. His flaming words have unique strength.

On the path up the mountain, the soul will meet and be tempted by false goods of many kinds. One by one they must be rejected in favor of the *nada*, nothingness. Faced successively with temporal advantages, intellectual riches, virtues the soul believes it possesses, graces, and finally self, the soul must give to all the same answer: Nothing, nothing, nothing, nothing, nothing.

This is a road nature [alone] cannot travel. Saint John of the Cross knows this well, so he draws the strength needed for detachment from an impassioned attachment to Christ. "If you desire to be perfect, sell your will, give it to the poor in spirit, come to Christ in meekness and humility, and follow him to Calvary and the sepulcher" (*Sayings*, #165). "If individuals resolutely submit to the carrying of the cross, ...they will discover in all [trials] great relief and sweetness. This will be so because they will be traveling the road denuded of all and with no desire for anything" (*Ascent*, 1, 7, 7).

To follow Christ does not mean, according to Saint John of the Cross, that one must in any way withdraw one's self from a system of human values or deny them by a renunciation of mind or senses. What he asks is that these values be used according to right order: the senses are to pass judgment on things of sense, the intellect is to appreciate things intellectual. It is only when one wishes to be united with and attain to God that these things must be renounced for the sake of faith, which henceforth is the only source of light, the only right path for this divine quest.

In two of his works, the *Ascent of Mount Carmel* and the *Dark Night,* John described the itinerary of the soul journeying towards the summits of divine union along the paths of renunciation; the first stresses the soul's work, while the second insists on the divine initiative.

Saint John of the Cross describes in terms of night the work accomplished first in the sensible part of the human person (this is the active and passive night of the senses); and then in the spiritual part (this is the active and passive night of the spirit). Here night is a symbol of the renunciation of things, a renunciation that is either voluntarily assumed or passively endured. The necessary role of the theological virtues is evident in the purification of the person's spiritual faculties: the intellect is purified by faith, the memory by hope, the will by charity. The light cast upon the role of the theological virtues, and especially on faith, is one of the most important aspects of Saint John's doctrine, and because of its universal value goes far beyond the limits of Carmelite spirituality.

What Saint John seeks is the path that leads quickly and surely to the summit of the mount of perfection and therefore to union with God. From this point of view the place he gives to faith is better understood. Its mission is to purify the soul's vision of God. In fact, it alone can remove whatever acts as a screen or an obstacle to the possession of God and enable us to see things truthfully, because faith is "an interior light derived from the light of God which illumines all things in the light of God and makes us see them as he does." [23]

There are two reasons why this light derived from God is a light of shadows. First, faith must cleanse our intellect of notions that are simply human and that are in no way worthy of God.

> It is noteworthy that among all creatures, both superior and inferior, none bears a likeness to God's being or unites proximately with him. Although truly, as theologians say, all creatures carry with them a certain relation to God and a trace of him, ...yet God has no relation or essential likeness to them. Rather the difference that lies between his divine being and their being is infinite. Consequently, intellectual comprehension of God through heavenly or earthly creatures is impossible; there is no proportion of likeness. (*Ascent*, 2, 8, 3)

This affirmation of the absolute divine transcendence, as well as the consequences that follow, is a keystone of the spirituality of Saint John and of Carmel. But if God is infinitely beyond our intellect, the soul "must journey, insofar as possible, by way of the denial and rejection of natural and supernatural apprehensions" (*Ascent*, 3, 2, 3). For the human intellect must enter into this night.

There is another reason why faith is "a light of shadows": it permits truth to be grasped only in darkness. Faith is a path "well suited for union with God" but this union is granted only "in a mirror and darkly."

Yet Saint John will sing its praises because "although it is night," it enables us to know God and to embrace him in the darkness.

> For I know well the spring that flows and runs,
> although it is night. (*Poems*, #8)

This grasp of the mystery of God by means of faith is limited only by our generosity. A faith absolutely freed from every image, from every representation, will give us God wholly.

> If the soul in traveling this road leans on any elements of its own knowledge or of its own experience or knowledge of God, it will easily go astray or be detained because it did not desire to abide...in the faith that is its guide. (*Ascent*, 2, 4, 3)

> People must empty themselves of all, insofar as they can, so that however many supernatural communications they receive, they will continually live as though denuded of them and in darkness. Like the blind, they must lean on dark faith, accept it for their guide and light, and rest on nothing of what they understand, taste, feel, or imagine. (*Ascent*, 2, 4, 2)

Discussing prayer, Saint John asks that this faith be exercised when he insists on the necessity of passing, at the prescribed time, from discursive meditation to the "obscure, general, loving" contemplation of the mystery of God (see *Ascent*, 2, 13, 4–7). It is plain that the faith he asks for is not theoretical or abstract but rich in love; it is a living faith.

Whence comes this faith? How is it strengthened in us? Here appears the magnificent synthesis that Saint John of the Cross achieves between the purest mysticism of Pseudo-Dionysius, negative and obscure, and the teaching that rightly gives priority of place to Christ in the spiritual life.

At no instant does Saint John of the Cross forget that Christ is "the author and finisher of our faith" (Heb 12:2). Christ gives us faith and he is the first to benefit from the gift. When the eyes of the soul are fixed on Christ, the Incarnate Word, faith enables them to discover him as he is, in the mystery of his divine and human Person. Before addressing the divine Persons of the Trinity and acquiring a "general, obscure, and confused" knowledge of God, faith turns first to Christ, and through faith the soul is in a certain sense made like him: "All of God's Wisdom is communicated in general, that is, the Son of God, who communicates himself to the soul in faith" (*Ascent*, 2, 29, 6).

To attain to God it is therefore essential to look with eyes illumined by faith, *fe ilustradísima* (*Flame*, 3, 80), upon him who is the way: "You will not find anything to ask or desire of me through revelations and visions. Behold him well, for in him you will uncover all of these already made and given, and many more.... Fix your eyes only on him and you will discern hidden in him the most secret mysteries, and wisdom, and wonders of God, as my Apostle proclaims: *In quo sunt omnes thesauri sapientiae et scientiae Dei absconditi* (In the Son of God are hidden all the treasures of the wisdom and knowledge of God)" (*Ascent*, 2, 22, 5–6).

Christ considered "in faith" becomes the door that introduces us into the mystery of divine life and the trinitarian exchanges. To Saint John of the Cross, as well as to the sacred writer, Christ is at the same time the author and finisher of our faith.

The path Saint John of the Cross follows in the purification of the memory by hope resembles the one he takes in the purification of the intellect by faith.

> Hope, also, undoubtedly puts the memory in darkness and emptiness as regards all earthly and heavenly objects. Hope always pertains to the unpossessed object. If something were possessed there could no longer be hope for it. (*Ascent*, 2, 6, 3)

And in the purification of the will by charity:

> Charity, too, causes a void in the will regarding all things since it obliges us to love God above everything. We have to withdraw our affection from all in order to center it wholly upon God. Christ says through St. Luke: *Qui non renuntiat omnibus quae possidet, non potest meus esse discipulus* (Whoever does not renounce all that the will possesses cannot be my disciple). (*Ascent*, 2, 6, 4)

> When the soul frees itself of all things and attains to emptiness and dispossession concerning them, which is equivalent to what it can do of itself, it is impossible that God fail to do his part by communicating himself to it, at least silently and secretly. It is more impossible than it would be for the sun not to shine on clear and uncluttered ground. As the sun rises in the

morning and shines on your house so that its light may enter
if you open the shutters, so God, who in watching over Israel
does not doze [Ps 121:4] or, still less, sleep, will enter the soul
that is empty, and fill it with divine goods. (*Flame*, 3, 46)

Union, the Transformation of the Soul in God by the Spirit of Love

If there is in the spiritual doctrine of Saint John of the Cross
a dark mountainside and a steep path of renunciation and faith for
the soul who ascends the mountain of Carmel in the footsteps of
Christ, there is also a summit of light awaiting the generous soul
who ascends with him. Saint John of the Cross describes and praises
this summit in his *Spiritual Canticle* and *Living Flame of Love*.

Nada, Todo. Nothing, Everything. The Doctor of nothingness
is even more admirable when he hymns the union of love with God,
its splendors and its joys. Of the "complete beatitude promised on
the mountain, he is the peerless doctor." [24] By poverty of spirit, by
faith, hope, and charity, Saint John has dug "deep caverns" in the
soul, infinite capacities that God longs to fill with this love "that he
has prepared for those who love him."

Desiring that other souls may benefit by what he himself has
experienced, the Mystical Doctor invites them to embark with him
upon this *dichosa ventura*, this "happy adventure." He urges them:
"Yours is all of this, and all is for you. Do not engage yourself in
something less" (*Sayings*, #27).

All this means God; all this means the whole Trinity. Does not
the Trinity dwell in the pure soul? Let the soul be conscious only of
this. Let it seek this divine Spouse who lives in the depths of its being and who invites it to be united with him.

> It should be known that the Word, the Son of God, to-
> gether with the Father and the Holy Spirit, is hidden by his
> essence and his presence in the innermost being of the soul.
> Individuals who want to find him should leave all things
> through affection and will, enter within themselves in deepest
> recollection, and let all things be as though not. (*Canticle*, 1, 6)

Recollection contains the seed of the whole mystical life. Saint

John of the Cross explains that this is because the author of this recollection is none other than the Holy Spirit, who:

> ...illumines the recollected intellect, and illumines it according to the mode of its recollection; the intellect can find no better recollection than in faith, and thus the Holy Spirit will not illumine it in any other recollection more than in faith. The purer and more refined a soul is in faith, the more infused charity it has. And the more charity it has the more the Holy Spirit illumines it and communicates his gifts because charity is the means by which they are communicated. (*Ascent*, 2, 29, 6)

In this way the mystical life is placed under the motion of the Spirit of Love from the very beginning. Christ does not cease to act in the soul by his Spirit. This Spirit purifies the soul along the paths ascending the Mount, detaches the soul during the trials of the nights, then floods the soul with light and love. Although the soul did not realize this, it was the influence of the Spirit that directed it and carried it toward the heights. On reaching the summits the soul perceives and knows itself to be entirely submissive to divine inspiration. The Holy Spirit, the Spirit of Jesus, is the great artisan of the mystical life, the master of the union of the soul with the Word its Spouse.

Although it is not necessary to have attained to mystical union in order to understand what Saint John of the Cross now has to say to us, still we must have some small experience of the secret action of the Holy Spirit in the soul. To those who have known this action, symbols and words themselves are eloquent. To those who lack this experience, these symbols and words fail to reveal the deep continuity of the action of the Holy Spirit and the unity that characterizes a life wholly marked with the Spirit's seal.

No doubt this unity can be explained, when the same image of divine action that was proposed by Saint John of the Cross in the *Ascent* is repeated in the first stanza of the *Living Flame*. And it is only when the soul can look back at the road it has traversed, and the transformation accomplished in it by this Spirit of multiple activities, that it becomes clearly aware of the power and admirable effects of divine Love.

Before the divine fire is introduced into the substance of the soul and united with it through perfect and complete purgation and purity, its flame, which is the Holy Spirit, wounds the soul by destroying and consuming the imperfections of its bad habits. And this is the work of the Holy spirit, in which he disposes it for divine union and transformation in God through love.

The very fire of love that afterward is united with the soul, glorifying it, is what previously assailed it by purging it, just as the fire that penetrates a log of wood is the same that first makes an assault on the wood, wounding it with the flame, drying it out, and stripping it of its unsightly qualities until it is so disposed that it can be penetrated and transformed into the fire. (*Flame*, 1, 19)

In this way the Holy Spirit enabled the soul to detach itself progressively from all things, buried it deep in faith, enlightened its darkness, helped it to go out of itself, brought it into the prayer of union to allow it to die interiorly and in pain cleansed it during the great passive purifcations of the nights. Now it is the Spirit who touches its inmost being with luminous and transforming fire. Throughout this whole work the soul never ceases to descend more deeply into its inner depths and to draw near this center from which it has its origin in God. Now this flame "transforms it into itself and gives it sweetness, peace, and light" (see *Flame*, 1, 23).

O living flame of love
that tenderly wounds my soul
in its deepest center!
Since now you are not oppressive,
now consummate! if it be your will:
tear through the veil of this sweet encounter!

To describe the action of the Holy Spirit and the graces given the soul, Saint John of the Cross has recourse in his poems to the "rich and burning words" [25] that the liturgy so often uses. In souls whom he is leading to transforming union, the Spirit is "the gentle breeze," the "unction," the "fire," the "perfume," the "living water." The Holy Spirit "breathes" through the garden of the soul, and each time that the Spirit touches the soul, "most delicately a knowledge full of serene and peaceful love" is communicated (see *Canticle*, 30, 1; *Flame*, 3, 43). The Spirit gives the soul the fragrance of divine sweetness as "the amber spreads its perfume" (*Canticle*, 18). But more than all else the Spirit is in the soul:

> ...not only as a fire that has consumed and transformed it but as a fire that burns and flares within it.... And that flame, every time it flares up, bathes the soul in glory and refreshes it with the quality of divine life. Such is the activity of the Holy Spirit in the soul transformed in love.... (*Flame*, 1, 3)

The soul is not only "entirely transformed by the divine flame," but it "has become a cautery of blazing fire" (*Flame*, 3, 2). Yet this vehement fire "does not consume or destroy the soul in which it so burns. And it does not afflict it; rather, commensurate with the strength of the love, it divinizes and delights it, burning gently within it" (*Flame*, 2, 3).

"O sweet cautery," cries the Mystical Doctor [in the poem "Living Flame of Love"], "O delightful wound! O gentle hand! O delicate touch!... O lamps of fire!...in your sweet breathing, filled with goodness and glory, how tenderly you swell my heart with love."

The action of the Holy Spirit is wholly concerned with the union of the soul with the Word, its Spouse. The [second redaction of the] *Spiritual Canticle* first describes the close of this painful night that prepares for the espousals and hints at "the waking of dawn" (stanzas 1–12); then the espousals themselves are described (stanzas 13–21); and lastly the spiritual marriage (stanzas 22–24). It is this marriage that gives the soul a very deep understanding of the inexhaustible mysteries of Christ and, by enabling the soul to live with the life of God himself, draws it into the bosom of the Trinity.

> By his divine breath-like spiration, the Holy Spirit elevates the soul sublimely and informs her and makes her capable of breathing in God the same spiration of love that the Father breathes in the Son and the Son in the Father. This spiration of love is the Holy Spirit himself, who in the Father and the Son breathes out to her in this transformation in order to unite her to himself. (*Canticle*, 39, 3)

The *Living Flame* also sings of "the most perfect and the richest love," of the soul united to God by love; it tries to describe the flaming of this love in the soul and it gives an analysis of the state of a soul that has reached this fullness of love. But when the Mystical Doctor begins to comment on the last stanza of his poem in which he sings of the mysterious awakening of God in the soul, overwhelmed then by "all the balsams and fragrant spices and flowers in the world," he pauses: "I do not desire to speak of this spiration, filled for the soul with good and glory and delicate love of God, for I am aware of being incapable of doing so; and were I to try, it might seem less than it is" (*Flame*, 4, 17).

In the soul united to Christ by the Spirit, in whom it has just been reborn, the great depths of Trinitarian life now open. But where Saint Teresa seems to see a goal that she contemplates, Saint John of the Cross finds a life with which he intends to nourish himself and which he intends to live in truth.

Saint Teresa writes in seventh dwelling place of the *Interior Castle:*

> When the soul is brought into that dwelling place, the Most Blessed Trinity, all three Persons, through an intellectual vision, is revealed to it through a certain representation of the truth..... Here all three Persons communicate themselves to it, speak to it, and explain those words of the Lord in the Gospel: that he and the Father and the Holy Spirit will come to dwell with the soul that loves him and keeps his commandments. (*Castle*, 7, 1, 6)

Going still further, Saint John declares, in all truth, but with remarkable daring:

> Thus the soul loves God with the will and strength of God himself, united with the very strength of love with which God loves her. This strength lies in the Holy Spirit.... (*Canticle*, 38, 3)

> For, granted that God favors [the soul] by union with the Most Blessed Trinity, in which she becomes deiform and God through participation, how could it be incredible that she also understand, know, and love—or better that this be done in

her—in the Trinity, together with it, as does the Trinity itself!
Yet God accomplishes this in the soul through communication
and participation. (*Canticle,* 39, 4)

It is evident that the riches poured by Saint John of the Cross
into Carmel's treasury are great. Contemplative souls never cease
to draw from this treasury. When the church made him a universal
"doctor" by giving him the title *Mystical Doctor,* contemplatives were
assured that they would find no guide more experienced, more
daring, more sure in every way, one who could lead them along the
paths of *Nothingness* to the possession of the *All* and the splendors
of divine union.

* * *

Under the impulse and *élan* given by Saint Teresa and Saint
John of the Cross, Carmel entered upon an era of prosperity and
could number souls of great value, skilled both in theory and practice.

The close of the sixteenth century and the seventeenth century are truly the golden age of the Reformed Carmel. They wit-
nessed the rapid multiplication of Carmelite houses for men and
women. In Spain the very name of *Salmanticenses* [a highly regarded
multivolume commentary on Aquinas written by Spanish Discalced
Carmelite theologians] suffices to testify to the intense intellectual
and theological activity of the order.

While John of Jesus-Mary, Thomas of Jesus, Joseph of Jesus-
Mary (Quiroga), Philip of the Trinity and, a little later, Joseph of
the Holy Spirit, studied the whole question of the mystical life, especially the difficult problem of acquired and infused contemplation, the *Reform of Touraine,* with the Venerable John of St. Samson,
strove to restore the primitive spirit of silence and solitude in all its
purity. The humble blind man of Rennes became the master and
director of a whole line of spiritual men [and women].

Toward the end of the seventeenth century, Brother
Lawrence of the Resurrection, a simple lay brother, the cook of the
convent of Rue de la Vaugirard [in Paris], brought back contemplative life to "the practice of the presence of God," returning in

this way to the primitive spirit of Elijah: "Yahweh lives in whose presence I stand." Lawrence said:

> In the ways of God...thought amounts to little, whereas love counts for everything. And it is not necessary...to have important things to do.... I flip my little omelette in the frying pan for the love of God, and when it's done, if I have nothing to do, I prostrate myself on the floor and adore my God who gave me the grace to do it, after which I get up happier than a king. When I can do nothing else, it is enough for me to pick up a straw from the ground for the love of God.
>
> We look for methods...to learn how to love God. We want to get there by I don't know how many practices. A multitude of methods makes it more difficult for us to remain in God's presence. Isn't it much shorter and more direct to do everyting for love of God, to use all the works of our state in life to manifest our love to him, and to foster the awareness of his presence in us by this exchange of our heart with him? Finesse is not necessary. We need only approach him directly and straightforwardly. (*Ways of Br. Lawrence*, 10)

But it is faith, and faith alone, that makes it possible for the soul to remain in this presence of God. Lawrence of the Resurrection extols the good results of this practice in these words:

> None of the fine speeches I hear about God, nothing I read or experience myself can satisfy me, for God is infinite in his perfections, and consequently ineffable, so there are no words powerful enough to give me a perfect idea of his grandeur. Faith reveals him to me and lets me know him as he is. I learn more by this means in a short time than I would learn in school in many years.... O faith! O faith! O admirable virtue that enlightens our minds and leads us to the knowledge of our Creator! It is faith that reveals to me the infinite perfections of God, that gives me a perfect idea of his greatness, that enables me to know him as he is. Faith teaches me in a short time more than I could ever learn in a long time in the schools. (*Eulogy for Br. Lawrence*, 43)

Nevertheless this faith has value in Lawrence's eyes only insofar as it is transformed into fire and kindles his love. "Everything is possible for one who believes, still more for one who hopes, even more for one who loves, and most of all for one who practices and perseveres in these three virtues" (*Maxims of Br. Lawrence,* 1)

Many of Saint Teresa's daughters, in their turn, attained to a high degree of prayer and spiritual life, and profoundly influenced the most enlightened and the most saintly souls of their age. For example, Blessed Marie of the Incarnation [Barbe Acarie] was venerated by all the mystics of Paris at the time of Bérulle and Saint Francis de Sales. The same is true of Anne of Jesus and Anne of St. Bartholomew, who came from Spain to establish foundations in France and then went to Belgium. At Beaune lived the humble Marguerite of the Blessed Sacrament.

The attraction of Carmel was also felt by the repentant soul of Louise de la Valliere who became Louise of the Mercy, and by the pure soul of Louise of France, the daughter of Louis XV, who thirsted for reparation.

Carmel flourished not only in France. In other lands as well the influence of Carmelites was very beautiful, especially in Florence, where Saint Mary Magdalene de' Pazzi lived, and a century later Saint Teresa Margaret Redi.

Yet beginning in the second half of the eighteenth century there was a sudden change that lasted for more than one hundred years. It would seem as if the mystics were silent or that they had no new message to give. Must the riches of the past henceforth suffice? Was Carmel asked to live on these treasures without adding anything more? To believe this would be to misunderstand completely the perpetual renewal that is the nature of contemplative life.

Does not the name of Elijah mean "the Verdant One"? A Saint Thérèse of the Child Jesus was to show the world that Carmel's vine continues to flower and bear fruit.

ST. THÉRÈSE OF THE CHILD JESUS AND THE HOLY FACE

Those who concentrate on the life and doctrine of this child of Carmel who died at the age of twenty-four are seized with wonder and admiration. They discover, in fact, that her contribution to spirituality is as original as it is profoundly traditional. They also discover that hidden under the Gospel-like simplicity of her message of "the little way of childhood" is a spiritual structure both strong and perfectly balanced from the theological point of view. No doubt this structure embodies the most authentic elements of the Order to which Thérèse belongs; but Thérèse has divided and arranged them according to her own genius. Better still, a very sure instinct, given by the Holy Spirit, enabled her to discern and sometimes to rediscover, not without merit, Carmel's purest spirit.

Saint Thérèse of the Child Jesus truly made this interior and radiant spirit incarnate. Her life of love of the absolute and of absolute love is of rare depth and fullness. It was a combination of certain interrelated spiritual principles and constitutes a true doctrine: this is "the little way of childhood" that we must now try to describe.

This doctrine is derived from a rediscovery of the central teaching of the Gospel, which may be expressed in this sentence: We are, in Christ, God's children, and we ought to love our Father in heaven with a filial love full of confidence and abandonment.

Christ taught us that God is our Father. Saint Thérèse adheres to this teaching with all her strength and gives to it its whole meaning. She had a deep understanding of the truth that such a teaching has two complementary aspects: a keen realization of God's fatherhood toward us; and the need for us to develop a filial attitude of absolute confidence toward God our Father.

If the confidence of Saint Thérèse in the goodness of her Father in heaven is absolute, this is because God is a father and this father is God. She comes to this basic affirmation: "We can never have enough confidence in God who is so good, so powerful, so merciful."

From this we can understand how, on her lips, the words "Papa the good God" (see *Story of a Soul,* p. 265; *Last Conversations,* p. 57) are not childish. On the contrary, they testify to the simplicity of her intimate relations with him and to a confidence so absolute that she can dare to say: "I know what it means to count on his mercy." [26]

One might be tempted to believe that such confidence was based on the assurance that had been given her that she "had never committed a mortal sin" (see *Story of a Soul,* p. 149). But she hastens to correct this idea: "Really tell them, Mother, that if I had committed all possible crimes, I would always have the same confidence; I feel that the whole multitude of offenses would be like a drop of water thrown into a fiery furnace" (*Last Conversations*, p. 89). "How can my confidence, then, have any limits?" (*Story of a Soul*, p. 200).

Saint Thérèse could certainly not have reached this point if she had not had a deep experience of God's love. Though she always claimed that she had not known extraordinary graces, and she never stressed the graces she did receive, it cannot be doubted that she had attained to a very high mystical life during a most painful night of faith.

But what might be misleading is that this mystical life was lived under the voluntarily obscure and detached sign of the little way of spiritual childhood. Wasn't Saint Thérèse eager to avoid anything that "little souls" could not imitate? What does this mean?

Saint Thérèse had very great desires, yet she would never admit that she was a great soul or that she had the strength necessary to do great things, like the saints who had been proposed to her as models. So she had to find a way in keeping with this littleness of which she was so deeply conscious.

More than this: she sought a way that depended on this very weakness. Had not the Apostle said: "When I am weak then I am strong" (2 Cor 12:10)? In searching the Gospels she found the words of the Master: "Let the little children come to me, and do not hinder them, for to such belongs the kingdom of heaven" (Mt 19:14).

Such a statement corresponded too well to her knowledge, both of her own weakness and of God's fatherly heart, for it not to have been a true light. It served, too, as a link between her spirit of childhood and her confidence in the divine fatherhood.

> Leaving to great souls, to great minds the beautiful books I cannot understand, much less put into practice, I rejoice at being little since children alone and those who resemble them will be admitted to the heavenly banquet. I am very happy there are many mansions in God's kingdom, for if there were only the one whose description and road seems incomprehensible to me, I would not be able to enter there. (*Correspondence*, LT 226, p. 1094)

This, therefore, was her way. God himself had pointed it out and declared its efficacy. On it Thérèse was to advance unfalteringly and to draw all the necessary conclusions with courage.

No one will deny that weakness is the characteristic of little children. But this weakness is the surest of guarantees to those who care for them and love them. Thérèse remembered a text of Isaiah that she copied in a little notebook she used: "As nurslings, you shall be carried in her bosom, and fondled in her lap. As a mother comforts her child, so will I comfort you" (Is 66:12).

Moreover, having learned from experience about this *motherly* goodness of God, and knowing that the smaller the child, the more it can count on merciful help and attentive care, Thérèse intended to remain little, that is to say, she would no more be concerned about her powerlessness; on the contrary she would rejoice in it. "How happy I am to realize that I am little and weak, how happy I am to see myself so imperfect." She does not count on her works, or on her merits, she "keeps nothing in reserve," and she is not to be discouraged even about her faults.

> [To remain a little child before God] is to recognize our nothingness, to expect everything from God as a little child expects everything from its father; it is to be disquieted about nothing, and not to be set on gaining our living. Even among the poor, they give the child what is necessary, but as soon as he grows up, his father no longer wants to feed him and says: "Work now, you can take care of yourself."
>
> It was so as not to hear this that I never wanted to grow up, feeling that I was incapable of making my living, the eternal life of heaven. I've always remained little, therefore, having no other occupation but to gather flowers, the flowers of love and sacrifice, and of offering them to God in order to please Him.
>
> To be little is not attributing to oneself the virtues that one practices, believing oneself capable of anything, but to recognize that God places this treasure in the hands of His little child to be used when necessary; but it remains always God's treasure. Finally, it is not to become discouraged over one's faults, for children fall often, but they are too little to hurt themselves very much. (*Last Conversations,* pp. 138–139)

This is a pleasant intuition and one that affords many fruitful applications for the spiritual life. Most especially it drew Thérèse along the path of a confidence that was not only a virtue but the life in us of the true theological virtue of hope. Advancing with great boldness to the end of this hope, and wishing to place no limits to God's mercy for those who love him with filial love, she wrote to a sister:

> You are not sufficiently trusting, you fear God too much. I assure you that this grieves him. Do not be afraid of going to purgatory because of its pain, but rather long not to go there because this pleases God who imposes this expiation so regretfully. From the moment that you try to please him in all things, if you have the unshakable confidence that he will purify you at every instant in his love and will leave in you no trace of sin, be very sure that you will not go to purgatory.[27]

And again:

> Oh! how you grieve me! You do a great injury to God in believing you're going to go to purgatory. When we love, we can't go there. (*Last Conversations*, p. 273)

> It seems to me, that for Victims of Love there will be no judgment. God will rather hasten to reward with eternal delights His own Love which He will behold burning in their hearts.[28]

Saint Thérèse's confidence in God's infinite mercy leads her to another certitude, as theologically sound as the preceding: that if God divides his graces unequally, he does so because of the same love.

> I wondered for a long time why God has preferences, why all souls don't receive an equal amount of graces.... Jesus deigned to teach me this mystery. He set before me the book of nature; I understood how all the flowers He has created are beautiful, how the splendor of the rose and the whiteness of the Lily do not take away the perfume of the little violet or the delightful simplicity of the daisy. I understood that if all flowers wanted to be roses, nature would lose her springtime beauty, and the fields would no longer be decked out with little wild flowers.

> And so it is in the world of souls, Jesus' garden....
> Our Lord's love is revealed as perfectly in the most simple
> soul that resists His grace in nothing as in the most excellent
> soul.... (*Story of a Soul*, p. 14)

Lastly, this confidence in God led Saint Thérèse, by paths of self-forgetfulness and poverty of spirit, to a wonderful simplification of the spiritual life. In fact, how could she have failed to notice that the kingdom of heaven is offered not only to little children but also to the poor in spirit, and almost in the same words: "Blessed are the poor in spirit, for theirs is the kingdom of heaven" (Mt 5:3). "Unless you turn and become like little children, you will not enter into the kingdom of heaven" (Mt 1 8:3). "Let the little children come to me, and do not hinder them, for of such is the kingdom of God" (Mk 10:14).

As Thérèse made spiritual childhood her own, so she made poverty of spirit her own. She aspired to be nothing more than "a poor little child" who looks to her Father for everything and who obtains everything from him because of this same poverty. She cultivated this poverty and wanted to keep nothing for herself, not even her merits and her good works.

> There is only one way to force the good God not to judge
> at all, and that is to present one's self to him with empty hands.
> (cf. *Counsels*, p. 242)

> ...When I think of these words of God: "My reward is with
> me, to render to each one according to his works" [Rev 22:12],
> I tell myself that He will be very much embarrassed in my case.
> I haven't any works! He will not be able to reward me "accord-
> ing to my works." Well, then. He will reward me "according to
> His own works." (*Last Conversations*, p. 43)

She is forgetful of herself and counts on nothing, she is truly poor: "It is necessary to consent to remain poor and weak; this is hard." "I have always longed to be unknown, I am resigned to being forgotten." "It is necessary to count on nothing."

Thérèse arrived at perfect detachment but in her own humble, hidden "little way."

Dear Sister, how can you say after this that my desires are the sign of my love?... Ah! I really feel that it is not this at all that pleases God in my little soul; what pleases Him is *that He sees me loving my littleness* and my *poverty, the blind hope that I have in His mercy....* That is my only treasure.... The weaker one is, without desires or virtues, the more suited one is for the working of this consuming and transforming Love. (*Correspondence,* LT 197, p. 999)

She buries herself with delight deep in this radical poverty. "I see it is sufficient to recognize one's nothingness and to abandon oneself as a child into God's arms" (*Correspondence,* LT 226, p. 1094).

Thérèse is marvelously free from herself and marvelously free for God. Her soul is wide open to the invasions of divine love. We, in fact, prevent God from coming to us and "flooding our souls with waves of his tenderness," because we do not open to him the place he wants to occupy. Only when poverty is united with confidence, is God able to realize in us the desires of his love. It is difficult for us to understand, much less describe, how great was Thérèse's desire to love. Yet she who wished "to love and to make Love loved," perhaps wished even more "to be loved" by this infinite Love. The deep reason for this will be evident when we remember that she wrote:

Merit does not consist in doing or in giving much, but rather in receiving, in loving much.... It is said, it is much sweeter to give than to receive, and it is true. But when Jesus wills to take *for Himself the sweetness of giving,* it would not be gracious to refuse. Let us allow Him to take and give all He wills. (*Correspondence,* LT 142, pp. 794–795)

To take and to give, in both cases, Thérèse will remain poor, in order that she can receive the love that God thirsts to pour out on her; she asks God "to consume me incessantly, allowing the waves of *infinite tenderness* shut up within You to overflow into my soul, and that thus I may become a *martyr* of *Your Merciful Love*" ("Act of Oblation to Merciful Love," in *Story of a Soul,* p. 277).

Because she will not keep this love for herself but will pour it out on others, she adds: "Were I to live to be eighty, I should always be poor, because I cannot economise. All my earnings are immediately spent on the ransom of souls" (*Counsels,* pp. 242–243).

Saint Thérèse was really flooded with divine love, and that is why her life bore such fruit. This charity transfigured two qualities that were always to remain united in her: love of God and love of neighbor. And when we consider her charity toward others, which was so practical, so delicate, so heroic—and flowed from a charity for God so faithful that "from the age of three she had never refused him anything" and was willing to suffer all things in silence for his love and for the love of souls—then no one can any longer oppose contemplation and action, prayer and the apostolate, the service of God and the service of the church.

She who had carried confidence and abandonment so far never ceased to multiply her own most concrete and generous efforts. It is because of this confidence and fidelity that God could communicate the plenitude of his own life that transformed her soul and opened it to the dimensions of infinite Love.

From the beginning of her religious life, Thérèse, like a true daughter of Elijah, is devoured with apostolic ardor. Wasn't it love for souls, especially the souls of priests, that brought her to Carmel? To save souls she would have liked to fulfill all vocations. She would have liked to have been preacher, apostle, missionary, martyr.

Yet it was only after she had offered herself to the divine outpouring and surrendered herself to Merciful Love that she discovered the vocation God destined for her.

> I understood that LOVE COMPRISED ALL VOCATIONS, THAT LOVE WAS EVERYTHING, THAT IT EMBRACED ALL TIMES AND PLACES....
> [My] vocation, at last I have found it...MY VOCATION IS LOVE!
> Yes, I have found my place in the Church and it is You, O my God, who have given me this place; in the heart of the Church, my Mother, I shall be *Love. (Story of a Soul,* p. 194)

It was only then, too, that her vocation reached its full apostolic dimension and revealed its limitless fruitfulness. In fact, henceforth, Thérèse was to think and to speak only in universal terms:

> Yes, I want to spend my heaven in doing good on earth....
> I can't rest as long as there are souls to be saved. But when the

angel will have said: "Time is no more!" then I will take my rest;
I'll be able to rejoice, because the number of the elect will be
complete and because all will have entered into joy and repose. (*Last Conversations,* p. 102)

Just as blood flows from the heart and moves with life-giving
power into every part of the whole body, so this apostolic spirit
springs from the love that possessed her and extends to the whole
church.

From her little cell, as from a broadcasting station, wonderful waves escape night and day. The souls whom they reach are
unaware of their origin. They merely murmur: "Someone has
prayed for me." [29]

Thérèse has given us the secret of this outpouring of love and
its apostolic fruitfulness: her love is crucified. In offering herself to
Merciful Love, she gave herself up without any reserve to trial and
suffering, which from that moment mark her life as with a seal.
From the day that "love penetrated and possessed her," suffering
seized her as if she were its prey. The victim offered in holocaust
had been accepted. Love was to consume her body, by a most painful illness, and her soul, by a terrible trial, "a wall which reaches
right up to the heavens and covers the starry firmament" (see *Story
of a Soul,* p. 214). "Never would I have believed it was possible to
suffer so much! never! never! I cannot explain this except by the
ardent desires I have had to save souls" (*Last Conversations,* p. 205).

But knowing that God had never before shown her so much
love, and that such trials also made it possible to prove her love for
him, Thérèse accepted them with heroic generosity and even with
joy. "I wouldn't want to suffer less" (*Last Conversations,* p. 230). She
offered her sufferings for souls until the last ounce of her strength:
"I am walking for a missionary" (*Last Conversations,* p. 262).

Before departing she gave us not only the assurance of a won-
derfully efficacious help ("Because I never did my will on earth, the
good God will do all that I want in heaven"), but she told us how
she was able to realize her contemplative and missionary vocation
in all its fullness: "I am not sorry for delivering myself up to Love"
[cf. *Last Conversations,* p. 205].

When we look at the life of Saint Thérèse of the Child Jesus we are struck by its simplicity and wonderful transparency. We are amazed to discover through her not only the purest Gospel teaching but Christ himself. We also notice that the unity of her spiritual life is unique and profound. In fact all her words, acts, sufferings, life, and death are of a piece, yield the same tone, and are proof of an equal plenitude. Like her Master, Thérèse is *true,* and also like him, her person and her message are one.

It should also be noted that the Christian instinct was not deceived. In search of a spirituality that is livable and adapted to life, thousands have turned to Saint Thérèse. Not the least original aspect of this cloistered religious who died at the age of twenty-four was that she gave to our times the most "incarnated" and at the same time the most supernatural doctrine there is. Transcendence and immanence. Her life prolongs the message of the Gospel in our midst. This, no doubt, is the reason that devotion to her, surprisingly enough, was not limited by the boundaries of France but became worldwide, truly universal because her spirit is truly Catholic.

Saint Thérèse brought a maximum depth and supernatural efficacy to the spiritual life. She is as apostolic as she is contemplative, and that with a minimum of means. Purely and simply, she succeeded in being both.

It is not only our utilitarian age (and this is true even in spiritual matters) that is conscious of her success. Christian life in general has been enriched by a new way leading to sanctity, a way as quick and sure as it is evangelical.

If Saint Thérèse received from Carmelite spirituality a great part of the wealth she used—and they are forgetful who fail to connect her with her "family" or minimize what she owes it—she knew how to increase her heritage. She offers us a style of spiritual life that is so detached, so simply reduced to the essentials, so supple in its absolute surrender to love, so generous in the gift to the church and to her sisters and brothers. She made her life a reality so near to us and so lived in God, that to breathe the fragrance of this flower of Carmel is to breathe the fragrance of eternal life.

St. Teresa of Avila (1515–1582)

St. John of the Cross (1542–1591)

V. Carmelite Prayer and Contemplation

The life and experience of Carmel's great saints enable us, better than all the theories, to understand the spirituality of the Order. So here we could stop. Yet, if we did, all that determines that spirituality—prayer and contemplation—might not be sufficiently clear.

Now a long experience of prayer has led Carmel to form, on this point, not a method but a doctrine. The ways of prayer, the nature of contemplation and of the mystical life, the problems they raise—all these were developed little by little thanks largely to the writings of Saint Teresa and Saint John of the Cross. The benefit to spirituality has been great. So it is fitting that we take a quick look at all this before we summarize, by way of conclusion, the characteristics of Carmelite spirituality.

Prayer

The passages in Sacred Scripture that concern the prophet Elijah have always symbolized contemplative and mystical life. "The Lord lives in whose presence I stand." "Hide yourself by the torrent of Carith." "When Elijah heard the whisper of a gentle breeze he covered his face with his mantle and went out to stand at the entrance to the cave." To this the *Institution of the First Monks* testifies, as we have seen. Besides the search for perfection, Carmel's first end, it indicates that there is a second one, no less essential: contemplation. "This end is communicated to us by God's pure gift." To drink of the torrent of divine pleasure is:

> ...to taste in our hearts and experience in our minds, not only after death but even during this mortal life, something of the power of the divine presence, and the bliss of heavenly glory. And this is to *drink from the brook* of the enjoyment of God....

Therefore contemplation is also one of Carmel's ends. Besides, it is only too evident that the central precept of the Rule, "to meditate day and night on the Law of the Lord," cannot mean *meditation* as opposed to *contemplation* [in the sense that these terms are sometimes understood today]. What the Rule prescribes is a *contemplative life* in which meditation and contemplation each has its own place. They must make it possible for the Carmelite to live constantly in God's presence.

Carmel has not only brought to the doctrine of prayer the riches of a long and wide experience. It also offers in the writings of its spiritual masters, Saint Teresa and Saint John of the Cross, a true summa of the ways of prayer.

Meditation

Carmel knows what meditation is and has a place for it. Saint John of the Cross speaks of meditation in the *Ascent* when he describes it as "a discursive act built on forms, figures, and images," as for example, "imagining Christ crucified or at the pillar or in some other scene" (*Ascent*, 2, 2, 12). Exercises like this are necessary for beginners.

Saint Teresa also speaks of meditation but praises it in only moderate terms. She says that this is a good way to begin (*Way*, 19, 1). She fears that meditation will detain souls in intellectual activity. What she praises much more is the prayer of active recollection. "But one should not always weary oneself in seeking these reflections but just remain there in His presence with the intellect quiet" (*Life*, 13, 22). This is a prayer "of recollection" because "the soul collects its faculties together and enters within itself to be with its God" (*Way*, 28, 4). "There is a withdrawing of the senses from exterior things and a renunciation of them in such a way that, without one's realizing it, the eyes close so as to avoid seeing them" and to enable the soul to awaken and see (*Way*, 28, 6).

This is "active" prayer because:

> ...it is something we can desire and achieve ourselves with the help of God.... This recollection is not a silence of the faculties; it is an enclosure of the faculties within the soul. (*Way*, 29, 5)

Then the soul:

> ...can think about the Passion and represent the Son and of-
> fer Him to the Father and not tire the intellect by going to look
> for Him on Mount Calvary or in the garden or at the pillar.
> (*Way,* 28, 4)

This retreat of the powers makes possible an intimacy with the
Master and an affectionate colloquy that are the heart of the prayer
of recollection. "Speak with Him as with a father, or a brother, or a
lord, or as with a spouse" (*Way,* 28, 3).

For Saint John of the Cross and for Saint Teresa, meditation
is directed toward simplification and interior silence. The soul has
to train herself to listen to what God says to her. She must recollect
herself. In this way she enters upon the path of contemplation.

Contemplation

Saint John of the Cross understands contemplation to be "a
general and loving attention to God." Intellect and will have their
share in this act, but it rests above all on a true connaturality with
God. It is both the highest activity of the soul and a passivity inspired by the Holy Spirit.

> ...They must learn to abide in that quietude with a loving at-
> tentiveness to God and pay no heed to the imagination and its
> work. At this stage, ...the faculties are at rest and do not work
> actively but passively, by receiving what God is effecting in
> them. If at times the soul puts the faculties to work, it should
> not use excessive efforts or studied reasonings, but it should
> proceed with gentleness of love, moved more by God than by
> its own abilities.... (*Ascent,* 2, 12, 8)

Therefore contemplation is a general and loving looking at
God. Now it springs from the whole work of the Mystical Doctor
that this looking and this knowing are the result of the light of faith
in the soul. Freed from sensory knowledge and from reasoning, the
soul begins to contemplate God in faith and to unite itself to him.

The Passage from Meditation to Contemplation

To advance from meditation to contemplation God must act
"with order, gently, and according to the mode of the soul" (*Ascent*,
2, 17, 3), beginning on the lowest step (and with the senses) so as
to lead the soul in this way to the highest level of spiritual wisdom
(which does not fall under the senses). The passage, strictly speak-
ing, will take place when "a simplified activity which is the fruit of
meditation" meets "an infusion of divine light." [30] The simplification of activity is, for the most part, the fruit of habit:

> It should be known that the purpose of discursive medita-
> tion on divine subjects is the acquisition of some knowledge
> and love of God. Each time individuals procure through medi-
> tation some of this knowledge and love they do so by an act.
> Many acts...will engender a habit....
> Accordingly the moment prayer begins, the soul, as one
> with a store of water, drinks peaceably without the labor and
> the need to fetch the water through the channels of past con-
> siderations, forms and figures. (*Ascent*, 2, 14, 2)

> ...God desires to liberate [beginners] from the lowly exer-
> cise of the senses and discursive meditation, by which they go
> in search of him so inadequately and with so many difficulties,
> and lead them into the exercise of spirit, in which they become
> capable of a communion with God that is more abundant and
> more free of imperfections.... Consequently, it is at the time
> they are going about their spiritual exercises with delight and
> satisfaction, when in their opinion the sun of divine favor is
> shining most brightly on them, that God darkens all this light
> and closes the door and the spring of sweet spiritual water they
> were tasting as often and as long as they desired.... God now
> leaves them in such darkness that they do not know which way
> to turn in their discursive imaginings. (*Night*, 1, 8, 3)

It is then that:

> God transfers his goods and strength from sense to spirit....
> Thus, while the spirit is tasting, the flesh tastes nothing at all
> and becomes weak in its work. But through this nourishment

the spirit grows stronger and more alert, and becomes more solicitous than before about not failing God.

If in the beginning the soul does not experience this spiritual savor and delight, but dryness and distaste, the reason is the novelty involved in this exchange. (*Night*, 1, 9, 4)

When can and should the passage from meditation to contemplation be prudently made? With great objectivity Saint John of the Cross lays down three signs that ought to be present simultaneously in the soul: first, the inability to meditate; and second, no inclination for anything particular, that is to say, for anything other than God.

The third and surest sign is that a person likes to remain alone in loving awareness of God, without particular considerations, in interior peace and quiet and repose, and without the acts and exercises (at least discursive, those in which one progresses from point to point) of the intellect, memory, and will. (*Ascent*, 2, 13, 4)

Like all deep transformations, this passage [from meditation to contemplation] is not instantaneous. Not only does the soul spend some time "in this vague realm where there is both activity and passivity, what is acquired and what is infused," but the soul must be humbly willing to return to meditation as often as is necessary. Nevertheless a moment will come when:

What the soul...was gradually acquiring through the labor of meditation on particular ideas has now, as we have said, been converted into habitual and substantial, general loving knowledge.... The moment it recollects itself in the presence of God it enters into an act of general, loving, peaceful, and tranquil knowledge, drinking wisdom and love and delight. (*Ascent*, 2, 14, 2)

So we see the psychology and delicacy with which the Mystical Doctor describes this prayer in which what is acquired is united with what is infused. The Teresian school always defended this prayer, using a term that caused much confusion—"acquired contemplation." In fact there is a whole set of dispositions that the soul ought to possess if she is to profit from the beginning of contemplation, and these dispositions should be taught.

This is what Saint John of the Cross did and what authors following Saint Teresa's teaching have done. Their doctrine is that of "active" or "acquired" contemplation. It would seem clearer to have used the terminology of the Mystical Doctor and to have taught that there is contemplation on the borderline of mystical experience, and that it is frequently granted to souls. In it the infusion of divine life meets simplified activity. But the light received is not sufficiently strong to steady and absorb the soul. So the soul must necessarily cooperate actively, lest it fall into quietism. This is "active-passive" contemplation and depends on both God and the soul, while infused contemplation strictly so-called depends on God alone.

Infused Contemplation and Mystical Union

When Saint John of the Cross and Saint Teresa speak of "contemplation," it is always "infused contemplation" to which they refer. They know no other.

For Saint Teresa, contemplation is a state that "we cannot bring about by ourselves. In it the soul feels passive." For Saint John of the Cross, contemplation is "an infused loving knowledge that both illumines and enamors the soul, elevating it step by step to God, its Creator" (*Night*, 2, 18, 5). The distinction between acquired and infused contemplation was not to be developed until later.

Aware, above all, of the passivity that accompanies supernatural recollection and mystical experience, Saint Teresa describes this supernatural recollection as a gradual taking possession of the faculties by God. A movement starting from the *center* of the soul where God dwells, takes possession of the will (the prayer of quiet) then of the intellect and imagination (this is the sleep of the faculties), so as to produce, by an ever greater deepening, complete passivity (prayer of union). Then the soul comes to the sixth dwelling places and reaches, with ecstasy, spiritual espousals.

In the seventh dwelling places she enjoys the fruits of union in spiritual marriage. During the espousals, divine life is only substituted from time to time for the soul's natural life (first five dwelling places); this happens more frequently (in the sixth dwelling places), and finally (in the seventh dwelling places) the union becomes permanent. Sometimes this union is experienced only in the depth of the soul, sometimes so powerfully in the whole person that one is lost in the contemplation of the divine Spouse. The passivity of the soul in these last dwelling places allows it now to say only "yes" to God.

Insofar as the soul dies to itself, it is born to a life infinitely higher and altogether divine. If it is willing to die totally, it will rise in God. "Since we do not succeed in giving up everything at once, this treasure [of divine love] as a result is not given to us all at once" (*Life*, 11, 2). Saint Teresa knew that this death and this life take place essentially by means of union of wills, and that ecstatic union is only its privileged manifestation.

However numerous and remarkable the extraordinary mystical facts described by the Saint, they never make her lose sight of the fact that they are only means of hastening the work of purification and of detaching the soul from itself so as to plunge it in God.

> True union can very well be reached, with God's help, if we make the effort to obtain it by keeping our wills fixed only on that which is God's will.... [If] you have obtained this favor from the Lord, ...you needn't care at all about the other delightful union....
>
> ...This union with God's will is the union I have desired all my life; it is the union I ask the Lord for always and the one that is clearest and safest. (*Castle*, 5, 3, 3–5)

Saint Teresa's teaching should be complemented and made more precise by that of Saint John of the Cross. The Mystical Doctor brightly illumined contemplative life and gave it new depth, especially by his description of the two nights: the night of the senses, which separates meditation from contemplation; and the night of the spirit, which is much more painful and precedes the prayer of union. The soul's powerlessness and emptiness, the knowledge it has acquired of its weaknesses, the feeling of being rejected by God forever, hasten and intensify this work of detachment and purification that condition the renewal of the soul's being and the infusion of graces and divine gifts.

It is less the succession of contemplative states (which largely coincide with those proposed by Saint Teresa) than the explanation of the principles of the soul's transformation that interests Saint John of the Cross. To him, progress in contemplation requires an intense life of the theological virtues. With the help of the gifts of the Holy Spirit, the soul passes from the human way of doing things to the divine; faith, hope, charity are seen to be the true principles of the soul's transformation and of its passage to the mystical life. This mystical life consists essentially of a *divinization* of soul. This means the divinization of the whole being through grace and the infused virtues, the divinization of all activity through the constantly deepening actualization of the gifts of the Holy Spirit.

The divine communication that acts only on the faculties and their operations allows at least some measure of spontaneity in the soul; but the communication that takes the form of a *substantial touch* reaches the very depths of the soul and reduces its powers to complete passivity. This *experience* of love is produced by a particularly deep divine movement and leads the soul to mystical marriage and perfect contemplation.

Perfect contemplation is made up of infused love and infused light; but these two elements are not given with equal intensity. Their complete communication is called the *substantial touch of divine union* (see *Ascent*, 2, 32, 5; *Night*, 2, 23, 11–12). The Mystical Doctor considers the theological virtues and the gifts of the Holy Spirit to be the fundamental principles of contemplation and the life of mystical union. But the *substantial touch* is the characteristic of perfect contemplation. "This is a touch of substances, that is, of the substance of God in the substance of the soul," and it "tastes of eternal life" (*Flame*, 2, 20–21).

We have spoken of the sureness and splendor with which Saint John of the Cross describes the unitive life, of the synthetic spirit with which he correlates all the elements of the mystical life with theological principles. In his writings light is never stressed at the expense of love. He is truly the Mystical Doctor *par excellence* and the inspired singer of divine love.

Contemplation and Perfection

Carmel is equally concerned about discovering what are the exact relations that unite mystical life and holiness, or contemplation and perfection. This concern is quite normal and is to be found in *The Institution of the First Monks,* as we have already observed.

> In regard to that life we may distinguish two aims, the one of which we may attain to, with the help of God's grace, by our own efforts and by virtuous living. This is to offer God a heart holy and pure from all actual stain of sin. This aim we achieve when we become perfect, and hidden in Cherith—that is in that charity of which the Wise One says: *Love covers all offenses.*
> The other aim of this life is something that can be bestowed upon us only by God's bounty: namely to taste in our hearts and experience in our minds, not only after death but even during this mortal life, something of the power of the divine presence, and the bliss of heavenly glory. And this is to *drink from the brook* of the enjoyment of God....
> The prophetic eremitical life must be undertaken by the monk with both both these ends in view....[31]

Therefore, if at Carmel, as in every religious life and even in every Christian life, the perfection of charity is to be sought before all else, then it would seem that infused contemplation must likewise be sought. Obviously it is impossible to secure this contemplation by oneself, but it is possible to prepare oneself for it. One may desire it, not explicitly but generally. Better still, one should tend toward it but not claim it as one's due. At Carmel, by the way of perfection the generous soul goes ahead, as it were, of the divine generosity, even, if it so please the divine Majesty, in the matter of contemplation.

So it is necessary that such souls be guided by wise directors who have had experience with contemplatives. Saint John of the Cross insists much both on this necessity and on the serious responsibility of those who, instead of leading souls along these steep paths, mislead them or prevent them from advancing. "These directors do not know what spirit is" (*Flame*, 3, 54). He deplores this kind of blindness, saying that:

> It is no light matter or fault to cause a soul to lose inestimable goods…. The affairs of God must be handled with great tact and open eyes, especially in so vital and sublime a matter as is that of these souls, where there is at stake almost an infinite gain in being right and almost an infinite loss in being wrong. (*Flame*, 3, 56)

Better than long arguments, these words of Saint John of the Cross show in what esteem divine union is held at Carmel. It is truly the precious pearl, for whose possession all the rest is well sacrificed. It is precious, not only for the soul itself, but still more for all souls who, because of the communion of saints, greatly benefit from this growth in love. "For a little of this pure love is more precious to God and the soul and more beneficial to the church, even though it seems one is doing nothing, than all these other works put together" (*Canticle*, 29, 2).

Conclusion

Characteristics of Carmelite Spirituality

"They were permitted, as they wished, to live in the perpetual service of the divine Master and his virgin Mother." ... These words [from the *Chronicle of William of Sanvico*] in fact describe Carmel's character and its object.[32] But we must also ask whether this double object, the service of God in prayer and the honor paid our Lady, is not itself understood in a way that is both general and yet specific.

Contemplation is a reality belonging to a well-defined order. It supposes, as Carmel has always understood, certain conditions of silence, solitude, recollection. It supposes, too, deep interior detachment. While Saint Teresa recalls that "whoever possesses God has all things, God alone suffices," Saint John of the Cross leads us to the summit of the mountain through a succession of *nothings*... "and on the mountain nothing." He exacts an integral, spiritual poverty, necessary to one who wishes to enter into the possession of the All.

John of St. Samson insists that one who wishes to live according to "the true spirit of Carmel" must live in a state of great purity. Madame Acarie often used to repeat: "Too avaricious is the soul for whom God does not suffice." Near to our own time, Sister Elizabeth of the Trinity writes:

> I think that in Heaven my mission will be to draw souls by helping them to go out of themselves in order to cling to God by a wholly simple and loving movement, and to keep them in this great silence within which will allow God to communicate Himself to them and to transform them into Himself." (L 335, see *Complete Works*, vol. 1, pp. 28–29)

Nakedness, detachment, poverty, nothingness, purity, simplicity.... In these words, traced so spontaneously by the pens of Carmelite authors and saints, an attempt is being made to express a profound reality. This is a reality whose demands the Carmelite soul feels deep within itself, longing as it does for total transparency, believing or knowing from experience that in no other way can God take possession of it.

> The soul on which the divine light of God's being is ever shining, or better, in which it is ever dwelling by nature, is like [a] window....
> A soul makes room for God by wiping away all the smudges and smears of creatures, by uniting its will perfectly to God's; for to love is to labor to divest and deprive oneself for God of all that is not God. When this is done the soul will be illumined by and transformed in God. (*Ascent,* 2, 5, 6–7)

In Carmel it is understood that purifications of soul and spiritual poverty are the necessary conditions for the possession of so great a good; they are, therefore, ardently sought. Of them may be said what the sacred writer says of wisdom: "All good things came to me together with her" (Wis 7:11).

It is indeed very remarkable that in Carmel, everything, including apostolic spirit, comes as a consequence of the divine possession of the soul.

Free, disencumbered, made simple, delivered from self-centered movements and unified by "the one thing necessary," the soul is now open to love.

> Now I occupy my soul
> and all my energy in his service;
> ....
> nor have I any other work
> now that my every act is love. (*Canticle,* 28)

Everything else flows from this. Surrendered to God, it places all its confidence in him, it abandons itself to him completely. Apostolic zeal and love of souls is the proof *par excellence* that the divine presence has kindled the heart.

Charity springs from the eremitical life, just as pure water rises in the oasis set in the midst of the desert. "I am on fire with zeal for the Lord of hosts."

élan = vigorous spirit or enthusiasm

Carmelite spirituality is not contemplative *and* apostolic. It is apostolic *because* it is contemplative. This is true because the soul is wholly subject to the action of the Holy Spirit. At every level of the spiritual life, the Holy Spirit is at work: purifying, enlightening, unifying, transforming. The Spirit is in the soul like an interior fountain, the source of its union with God. Is he not the Spirit of Love? Guided by the Holy Spirit, the soul acquires great simplicity in its abandonment to the divine action, an awareness of a living, spiritual continuity, as well as a constantly renewed *élan*.

The Holy Spirit is the source of contemplative life as well as the life of the apostolate. It is the Spirit who draws us into himself for prayer and sends us out to conquer the world. The Spirit of the Cenacle is also the Spirit of Pentecost: "you shall send forth your Spirit, and they shall be created, and you shall renew the face of the earth."

It is in this perspective of simplicity, detachment, and unity that Carmel envisages our Lady. Carmel sees in her the "soul" in the presence of God. Her purity and simplicity are ravishing. She is the soul whom God has completely and absolutely unified. In her is admirably made manifest the omnipotence of the Spirit, the origin of contemplation, and the origin of the apostolate.

Through Mary, Carmel perceives the ideal toward which it is drawn and which attracts it. This is a life of unity in God, of union with Christ, of efficacious and salvific charity toward all people.

Of course, for Carmel as for every Christian soul, Mary is above all the Mother. "She is more mother than queen," affirms Saint Thérèse of the Child Jesus. But she is also something more. She is "the beauty of Carmel." What does that mean? Under this mysterious title, Carmel tries to express something of what she means to the Order: a brightness of eternal light, she in whom God allows himself to be contemplated and cherished, she in whom "the divine light knows no shadow."

Now we understand why, at Carmel, at least for certain souls, Mary is intimately associated with the very practice of contemplation. In her the Lord has done great things. The purity and transparency of her soul enables us to see God at work in her and to contemplate in her a reflection of the divine Beauty.

This soul, so transparent, is, we know, that of our mother. Her mission is to form us to live a life of union with God such as she enjoyed. How could our path not lead us to her? So we see that at Carmel there has always been a contemplative way on which union with Mary, far from being an obstacle, or even a detour, is envisaged as an essential condition for advancing to the highest mystical life.

> The soul discovers that Marian contemplation does not lead her away from adhesion to or immediate union with the Sovereign Good and the simple essence of God considered in itself. On the contrary the soul finds herself attracted to God with greater facility and is held by him with greater stability.... All this is effected in the soul by one and the same Spirit, the author of this Marian life which leads finally to a perfectly mystical life.[33]

This, then, is Carmelite spirituality: an attraction for open spaces and solitude, interior liberty, simplicity, and unity under the impulse of the Spirit of Love.

Such a spirituality requires a fundamental grasp of the absolute that lifts the soul out of itself and leads it to the heights. The absolute of divine transcendence is the basis of the soul's adoration and introduces Carmel to purest theocentrism: "I shall keep my strength for You alone" (Ps 59:10).[32] The absolute of love requires that all things be sacrificed for love and that all things be changed into love. "Where there is no love, put love, and you will draw out love" (John of the Cross, *Letters*, #26).

Vowed to the service of Love, the soul is not satisfied with loving but seeks to experience love, to suffer love, and at last to be transformed into love.

Although Carmelite spirituality gives the soul the liberty and simplicity of the children of God and leads it to the heights, it also requires that all this be constantly examined in the light of principles of wisdom, of most judicious psychology and of "discretion." Finally, it weighs mysticism itself in the Gospel scales of wholesome and supernatural realism. "Whoever has my commandments and observes them is the one who love me.... Those who love me will keep my word, and my Father will love them, and we will come to them and make our dwelling with them" (Jn 14: 21, 23).

Carmelite spirituality is immanent and transcendent. To an *élan* toward the summits it brings a deep psychological insight and a keen realism. That is why during all these centuries it has been able to guide souls to the top of the holy mountain. In spite of their wide diversity, Carmel makes it possible for all souls to realize their highest and most necessary vocation: *Vivere Deo*—To live for God.

St. Thérèse of Lisieux (1873–1897)

Notes

1. Jérôme de la Mère de Dieu, O.C.D., quoting Costa Rosetti, S.J. in "La doctrine du venerable frère Jean de S. Samson," *La Vie Spirituelle* (1925): 32, note 1.

2. Saint John of the Cross gives a startling confirmation of this fact when he recalls it in the very opening words the *Ascent of Carmel.* There he writes: "This treatise explains how to reach divine union quickly."

3. *The Book of the Institution of the First Monks (Chapters 1 to 9),* Introduced and Translated by Bede Edwards, O.C.D. (Boars Hill, Oxford: Teresian Press, 1969), pp. 3–4.

4. [Most contemporary historians now date the beginnings of the Latin hermits of Mount Carmel (who were to become the Carmelites) from some time after the Battle of Hattin in 1187. The monks described by John Phocas were probably Greek; moreover, their community near the cave of Elijah ("El-Chadr") was in fact some distance from the fountain of Elijah where the Carmelites established themselves. See Elias Friedman, *The Latin Hermits of Mount Carmel: A Study in Carmelite Origins* (Rome: Teresianum, 1979); Joachim Smet, *The Carmelites: A History of the Brothers of Our Lady of Mount Carmel,* vol. 1: *Ca.1200 A.D. until the Council of Trent* (Darien, IL: Carmelite Spiritual Center, 1975).—Ed.]

5. [From the text of the Rule as given in the current *Constitutions and Norms* of the Discalced Carmelite friars (Dublin, 1988). This translation can also can be found in *The Rule of St. Albert,* trans. Bede Edwards (Aylesford and Kensington, 1973), para. 2. Another translation is included in *Albert's Way,* ed. Michael Mulhall (Rome: Institutum Carmelitanum, 1989). Albert of Vercelli did not become Latin Patriarch of the Holy Land until 1206, and he was assassinated in 1214, so 1209 is often chosen as an approximate date for the original text of his "Rule" or "formula of life" for the Carmelites.—Ed.]

6. John of St. Samson, *Le vrai esprit du Carmel [The True Spirit of Carmel],* 1658.

7. François de Sainte-Marie, *La Règle du Carmel et son esprit* (Paris: Édition du Seuil, 1949), p. 33.

8. Rule of St. Albert, from the *Constitutions and Norms* of the Discalced Carmelite friars.

9. François de Sainte-Marie, p. 88.

10. First *Constitutions* of Italy.

11. François de Sainte-Marie, p. 112. [In fact the *Book of the Institution of the First Monks* traces the historical origins of the Carmelite Order back to Elijah, and interprets allegorically the small cloud observed by Elijah's servant (see 1 Kgs 19:44), as a foreshadowing of the torrent of grace to come through Mary. Later generations of Carmelites spent much time and energy trying, with diminishing success, to defend these historical and exegetical claims. Most today, however, approach *The Book of the Institutions of the First Monks* not as a work of history but as treasury of medieval Carmelite spirituality.—Ed.]

12. See John Grossi, *Viridarium* (after 1411). [The first surviving account of the Scapular vision did not appear until about a century and a half after 1251, the traditional date of the event. Moreover, it now appears that the first General of the Carmelites, who would have been in office in 1251, was a man named Godfrey. A saintly "Simon," honored in the current Carmelite calendar as "Simon Stock," was elected only later, in 1256. Though not disproving that some vision related to the Scapular occurred in that period, these recent findings create serious difficulties for the traditional chronology. Consequently, Carmelites today are more inclined to emphasize that the Scapular devotion, whatever its precise origins, has been amply approved and encouraged by the church, as a way of expressing allegiance to Mary and confidence in her protection by wearing a portion of the habit of the Order dedicated to her honor. See Smet, *The Carmelites*, vol. 1, pp. 26ff.; Gabriel Barry, *Historical Notes on the Carmelite Order*, (Darlington Carmel, n.d.), pp. 73–78.—Ed.]

13. Elisée de la Nativité, "La vie mariale au Carmel," *Maria* (II): 839.

14. [Contrary to what is sometimes popularly assumed, the level of religious observance was comparatively high among the Carmelites of Castile at the time of the Teresian Reform, and the Castilian province was regarded as one of the more "observant" in the Order. See Federico Ruiz et al., *God Speaks in the Night: The Life,*

Times, and Teaching of St. John of the Cross, trans. Kieran Kavanaugh (Washington, DC: ICS Publications, 1991), pp. 60, 120–123. Teresa herself insists that the Carmel of the Incarnation, which she left to make her first foundation, included many dedicated and holy nuns. Perhaps it is fairer to say, then, that Teresa and John were not so much fleeing an Order in spiritual decay as seeking a renewed form of Carmelite community more effectively structured to support the kind of intense life of contemplative prayer, inspired by the *Rule* of St. Albert, that Teresa envisioned.—Ed.]

　　15. Marcel Lépée, *Sainte Thérèse d'Avila: Le réalisme chrétien* (Paris: Desclée de Brouwer, 1947). This is a volume in the series *Études Carmélitaines.*

　　16. Gabriel of St. Mary Magdalen, "Carmes," in *Dictionnaire de Spiritualité,* col. 197.

　　17. Lépée, p. 154.

　　18. Lépée, p. 172.

　　19. Francisco Ribera, *La Vida de la Madre Teresa de Jesús...,* new ed., with introduction, notes and appendices by P. Jaime Pons (Barcelona: Gustavo Gili, 1908), II, ch. 1.

　　20. [Although good works are done most perfectly, and with the least self-interest, once one reaches union with God, neither John nor Teresa would claim that we should postpone opportunities for doing good until we have reached mystical union. The author's point seems to be rather that we should be careful not to let our activism and apostolic efforts become an excuse for avoiding the transformative power of contemplative prayer.—Ed.]

　　21. Lucien-Marie de Saint-Joseph, O.C.D., Introduction to *Les Oeuvres Spirituelles du Bienheureux Père Jean de la Croix,* trans. Cyprien de la Nativité (Bruges: Desclée de Brouwer, 1942), p. 31.

　　22. Joannes Wehrlé, *La vie et la doctrine de Saint Jean de la Croix* (Paris, 1925).

　　23. Yves Congar, *The Mystery of the Church: Studies,* trans. A. V. Littledale (Baltimore, MD: Helicon Press, 1960), p. 124.

　　24. Dom Chevalier, *Le Cantique Spirituel de Saint Jean de la Croix docteur de l'Église: Notes historiques, text critique, version française* (Bruges: Desclée de Brouwer, 1930), p. XXXIV.

　　25. François de Sainte-Marie, *Initiation à Saint Jean de la Croix* (Paris: Éditions du Seuil, 1954) p. 175.

26. [As indicated on pp. 7–8, Readers should be aware that Père Paul-Marie frequently quotes (without giving chapter or page number) from the earliest edition of *l'Histoire d'une Âme,* because the critical French edition, from which the ICS edition was translated, was not yet available at the time he wrote. This earlier edition, extensively edited by Thérèse's sister Pauline (Mother Agnes), contains a section of "Counsels and Reminiscences." An English translation, with the "Counsels," may be found in *Soeur Thérèse of Lisieux, the Little Flower of Jesus: A New and Complete Translation of "Histoire d'une Âme"...,* trans. Thomas N. Taylor (New York: P. J. Kenedy & Sons, 1912); quotations from the Taylor translation are indicated by the word "Counsels" together with the page number in his edition.—Ed.]

27. Extract of a circular letter from Lisieux signed by Rev. Mother Agnes, February 17, 1924.

28. Quoted in Taylor, p. 243; cf. *Correspondence,* LT 226.

29. Abbé Thellier de Poncheville.

30. Gabriel of St. Mary Magdalene, col. 182.

31. *Book of the Institution of the First Monks,* chap. 2.

32. [The *Chronicle of William of Sanvico,*proportedly a 13th century account of the Carmelites' expulsion from Mt. Camel and migration to the West, was included with the *Book of the Institution of the First Monks* and other documents in Philip Ribot's *De institutione et pecularibus gestis Carmelitarum* (1370). Smet observes that "lately the considered judgment [of scholars]…is that these works do not antedate their publication by Ribot" (see Smet, vol. 1, p. 64). Even so, they remain important medieval expressions of the Carmelite self-understanding and ideal.—Ed.]

33. Michael of St. Augustine, *De vita Maria-forme et mariana.* English translation by Thomas McGinnis in *Life With Mary: A Treatise on the Marian Life* (New York: Scapular Press, 1953). Michael of St. Augustine was, as we know, the director of the Carmelite tertiary and mystic, Marie (Petyt) de Sainte-Thérèse (d. 1677), and his works were strongly influenced by the experiences of this Flemish recluse.

34. In four places (*Ascent,* 1, 10, 1; 3, 16, 1; *Night,* 2, 11, 3; *Canticle,* 28, 8) Saint John of the Cross quotes this verse; see also the commentary on *Canticle A,* 19, 7.

Select Bibliography
of Related Works in English

I. General Introductions

Barry, Gabriel. *Historical Notes on the Carmelite Order.* Darlington, England: n.d.

Brandsma, Titus. *Carmelite Mysticism: Historical Sketches.* 50th anniversary edition. Darien, IL: Carmelite Press, 1986.

Payne, Steven. "The Tradition of Prayer in Teresa and John of the Cross." In *Spiritual Traditions for the Contemporary Church,* ed. Robin Maas and Gabriel O'Donnell, pp. 235–258. Nashville, TN: Abingdon, 1990.

Rohrbach, Peter-Thomas. *Journey to Carith: The Story of the Carmelite Order.* Garden City, NY: Doubleday, 1966.

Saggi, Louis, ed. *Saints of Carmel.* Rome, Italy: Carmelite Institute, 1972.

Slattery, Peter. *The Springs of Carmel: An Introduction to Carmelite Spirituality.* Staten Island, NY: Alba House, 1991.

Smet, Joachim. *The Carmelites: A History of the Brothers of Our Lady of Mount Carmel.* 4 vols. Darien, IL: Carmelite Spiritual Center, 1975–1985.

Stein, Edith. "On the History and Spirit of Carmel." In *The Hidden Life: Hagiographic Essays, Meditations, Spiritual Texts.* Washington, DC: ICS Publications, 1992.

Valabek, Redemptus Mary. *Prayer Life in Carmel.* Rome: Institutum Carmelitanum, 1982.

Welch, John. *The Carmelite Way: An Ancient Path for Today's Pilgrim.* New York: Paulist Press, 1997.

II. Origins and Medieval Period

Barry, Gabriel. *The Inspiration of Carmel.* Vineyard Series 1. Durham, England: Teresian Press, 1984.

Cicconetti, Carlo. *The Rule of Carmel.* Darien, IL: Carmelite Spiritual Center, 1984.

Edwards, Bede, trans. *The Book of the First Monks (Chapters 1 to 9).* Durham, England: Teresian Press, 1969.

Edwards, Bede, trans. *The Rule of St. Albert.* Aylesford and Kensington: Carmelite Press, 1973.

Egan, Keith. "The Spirituality of the Carmelites." In *Christian Spirituality,* Vol. 2: *High Middle Ages and Reformation,* ed. Jill Raitt, pp. 50–62. New York, NY: Crossroad, 1987.

Friedman, Elias. *The Latin Hermits of Mount Carmel: A Study in Carmelite Origins.* Rome: Teresianum, 1979.

Merton, Thomas. "The Primitive Carmelite Ideal." In *Disputed Questions,* pp. 204–249. New York, NY: Farrar, Straus and Giroux, Noonday Press, 1960.

Mulhall, Michael, ed. *Albert's Way: First North American Congress on the Carmelite Rule.* Rome: Institutum Carmelitanum, 1989.

Nicholas of Narbonne. *The Flaming Arrow.* Trans. Michael Edwards. Vineyard Series 2. Durham, England: Teresian Press, 1985.

Werling, Norman G., trans. "The book of St. John, 44." in *Sword* 4 (January, 1940): 25–34.

III. Teresa and the Teresian Reform

Alvarez, Tomas (of the Cross). "The Carmelite School: St. Teresa and St. John of the Cross." In *Jesus in Christian Devotion and Contemplation,* trans. Paul Oligny. St. Meinrad, IN: Abbey Press, 1974. Pp. 86–101, 111–113.

Alvarez, Tomas and Domingo, Fernando. *Saint Teresa of Avila: A Spiritual Adventure,* trans. Christopher O'Mahoney. Washington, DC: ICS Publications, 1982.

Auclair, Marcelle. *Teresa of Avila.* Garden City, NY: Doubleday Image, 1953. [Reprinted by St. Bede's, Petersham, MA.]

Bielecki, Tessa. *Holy Daring: An Outrageous Gift to Modern Spirituality from Saint Teresa, the Grand Wild Woman of Avila.* Rockport, MA: Element, 1994.

Bilinkoff, Jodi. *The Avila of St. Teresa.* Ithaca, NY: Cornell University Press, 1989.

Brice, Rev. *Teresa, John and Thérèse.* New York, NY: Frederick Pustet Co., 1946.

Burrows, Ruth. *Interior Castle Explored.* London: Sheed & Ward, 1982.

Carmelite Studies, vols. 1–6. Washington, DC: ICS Publications.

Chorpenning, Joseph. *The Divine Romance.* Chicago, IL: Loyola University Press, 1992.

Clissold, Stephen. *St. Teresa of Avila.* New York, NY: Seabury Press, 1982.

Dicken, E. W. Trueman. *The Crucible of Love: A Study of the Mysticism of St. Teresa of Jesus and St. John of the Cross.* New York, NY: Sheed & Ward, 1963.

Dubay, Thomas. *Fire Within: St. Teresa of Avila, St. John of the Cross and the Gospel on Prayer.* San Francisco, CA: Ignatius Press, 1989.

Du Boulay, Shirley. *Teresa of Avila: Her Story.* Ann Arbor, MI: Servant Publications, 1991.

Egan, Harvey. *Christian Mysticism.* New York, NY: Pueblo Publishing, 1984. Chap. 4.

Egido, Teofanes. "The Historical Setting of St. Teresa's Life." In *Carmelite Studies,* vol. 1. Washington, DC: ICS Publications, 1980. Pp. 122–182.

Galilea, Segundo. *The Future of Our Past: The Spanish Mystics Speak to Contemporary Spirituality.* Notre Dame, IN: Ave Maria Press, 1985.

Haneman, Mary Alphonsetta. *The Spirituality of St. Teresa of Avila.* Boston, MA: St. Paul Editions, 1983.

Kavanaugh, Kieran. "St. Teresa and the Spirituality of Sixteenth Century Spain." In *The Spirituality of Western Christendom,* Vol. 2: *The Roots of the Modern Christian Tradition,* ed. E. Rozanne Elder. Kalamazoo, MI: Cistercian Publications, 1984.

_____. "Spanish Sixteenth Century: Carmel and Surrounding Movements." In *Christian Spirituality, Vol. 3: Post-Reformation and Modern,* ed. Louis Dupré and Don E. Saliers, pp. 69–92. New York, NY: Crossroad, 1991.

Lavelle, Louis. *The Meaning of Holiness.* New York, NY: Pantheon Books, 1954.

Madeleine of St. Joseph. *Within the Castle With St. Teresa of Avila.* Chicago, IL: Franciscan Herald Press, 1982.

Luti, J. Mary. *Teresa of Avila's Way.* Collegeville, MN: Liturgical Press, 1991.

Marie-Eugene. *I Want to See God* and *I Am a Daughter of the Church.* Westminster, MD: Christian Classics, 1982.

Moriones, Ildefonso. *The Teresian Charism: A Study of the Origins.* Rome: Teresianum, 1968.

O'Donoghue, Noel Dermot. *Mystics for Our Time: Carmelite Meditations for a New Age.* Collegeville, MN: Michael Glazier Book, Liturgical Press, 1989. Chaps. 6–4.

Peers, E. Allison. *Mother of Carmel: A Portrait of St. Teresa of Jesus.* Wilton, CT: Morehouse-Barlow, 1979.

Rohrbach, Peter-Thomas. *Conversation With Christ.* Rockford, IL: TAN Books, 1980.

Teresa of Jesus, St. *The Collected Works of St. Teresa of Avila,* trans. Kieran Kavanaugh and Otilio Rodriguez. 3 vols. Washington, DC: ICS Publications, 1976–1985.

_____. *The Complete Works of St. Teresa of Avila,* trans. E. Allison Peers. 3 vols. London: Sheed & Ward, 1972.

_____. *The Letters of St. Teresa of Avila,* trans. E. Allison Peers. 2 vols. London: Sheed & Ward, 1980.

Walsh, William Thomas. *Saint Teresa of Avila.* Rockford, IL: TAN Books, 1987.

Weber, Alison. *Teresa of Avila and the Rhetoric of Femininity.* Princeton, NJ: Princeton University Press, 1990.

Welch, John. *Spiritual Pilgrims: Carl Jung and Teresa of Avila.* Mahwah, NJ: Paulist Press, 1982.

Williams, Rowan. *Teresa of Avila.* Wilton, CT: Morehouse Publishing, 1992.

Word & Spirit: A Monastic Review. Vol. 4. Still River, MA: St. Bede's Publications, 1983.

IV. John of the Cross

Ahern, Barnabas. "The Use of Scripture in the Spiritual Theology of St. John of the Cross," *Catholic Biblical Quarterly* 14 (1952): 6–17.

Arraj, James. *St. John of the Cross and Dr. C. G. Jung.* Chiloquin, OR: Tools for Inner Growth, 1986.

Brenan, Gerald. *St. John of the Cross: His Life and Poetry.* With a translation of his poetry by Lynda Nicholson. Cambridge: Cambridge University Press, 1973.

Bruno de Jesus-Marie. *Saint John of the Cross.* New York, NY: Sheed & Ward, 1932.

Burrows, Ruth. *Ascent to Love: The Spiritual Teaching of St John of the Cross.* Denville, NJ: Dimension Books, 1987.

Collings, Ross. *John of the Cross.* Way of the Christian Mystics Series, 10. Collegeville, MN: Michael Glazier Book, Liturgical Press, 1990.

Crisógono de Jesús Sacramentado. *The Life of St. John of the Cross.* Trans. Kathleen Pond. London: Longmans, Green & Co., 1958.

Cugno, Alain. *Saint John of the Cross: Reflections on Mystical Experience.* Translated by Barbara Wall. New York, NY: Seabury Press, 1982.

Cummins, Norbert. *Freedom to Rejoice: Understanding St John of the Cross.* San Francisco, CA: Harper & Row, 1992.

Doohan, Leonard. *The Contemporary Challenge of John of the Cross: An Introduction to His Life and Teaching.* Washington, DC: ICS Publications, 1995.

Egan, Harvey. *Christian Mysticism.* New York, NY: Pueblo Publishing, 1984. Chap. 5.

Egan, Keith J. "The Symbolism of the Heart in John of the Cross." In *Spiritualities of the Heart,* edited by Annice Callahan. Mahwah, NJ: Paulist Press, 1990.

FitzGerald, Constance. "Impass and Dark Night," in Tilden Edwards, ed. *Living With Apocalypse: Spiritual Resources for Social Compassion.* San Francisco, CA: Harper & Row, 1984. Pp. 93–116.

Foresti, Fabrizio. *Sinai & Carmel: The Biblical Roots of the Spiritual Doctrine of St. John of the Cross and Three Other Biblical Conferences.* Darlington Carmel, England: Darlington Carmel, 1981.

Gaudreau, Marie M. *Mysticism and Image in St. John of the Cross.* New York, NY: Peter Lang, 1976.

Giallanza, Joel. "Spiritual Direction According to St. John of the Cross." *Contemplative Review* 11 (Fall, 1978): 31–37.

Giles, Mary. *The Poetics of Love: Meditations With John of the Cross.* New York, NY: Peter Lang, 1986.

Graviss, Dennis. *Portrait of the Spiritual Director in the Writings of St. John of the Cross.* Rome: Institutum Carmelitanum, 1983.

Green, Thomas. *When the Well Runs Dry: Prayer Beyond the Beginnings.* Notre Dame, IN: Ave Maria Press, 1979.

Hardy, Richard P. *The Search for Nothing: The Life of John of the Cross.* New York, NY: Crossroad, 1982.

John of the Cross. *The Complete Works of Saint John of the Cross,* translated and edited by E. Allison Peers, from the critical edition of P. Silverio de Santa Teresa, new ed., rev., 3 vols. Westminster, MD: Newman Press, 1957.

_____. *The Collected Works of St. John of the Cross,* translated by Kieran Kavanaugh and Otilio Rodriguez, rev. ed. by Kieran Kavanaugh. Washington, DC: ICS Publications, 1991.

_____. *John of the Cross: Selected Writings.* Edited and with an introduction by Kieran Kavanaugh. Preface by Ernest Larkin. Classics of Western Spirituality Series. Mahwah, NJ: Paulist Press, 1987.

Lyddon, Eileen. *Door Through Darkness: John of the Cross and Mysticism in Everyday Life.* Hyde Park, NY: New City Press, 1995.

Matthew, Iaian. *The Impact of God: Soundings from St John of the Cross.* London: Hodder & Stoughton, 1995.

Merton, Thomas. *The Ascent to Truth.* New York, NY: Harcourt, Brace & Co., 1951.

_____. "Light in Darkness: The Ascetical Doctrine of St. John of the Cross." In *Disputed Questions,* pp. 194–203. New York, NY: Farrar, Straus & Giroux, Noonday Press, 1976.

Muto, Susan. *John of the Cross for Today:* The Dark Night. Notre Dame, IN: Ave Maria Press, 1994.

_____. *John of the Cross for Today:* The Ascent. Notre Dame, IN: Ave Maria Press, 1991.

_____. *Words of Wisdom for Our World: The Precautions and Counsels of St. John of the Cross.* Washington, DC: ICS Publications, 1995.

Nemick, Francis Kelly and Coombs, Marie Theresa. *O Blessed Night: Recovering from Addiction, Codependency and Attachment based on the insights of St. John of the Cross and Pierre Teilhard de Chardin.* Staten Island, NY: Alba House, 1991.

O'Donoghue, Noel Dermot. *Lovlier Than the Dawn: Four Meditations on the Mystical Teachings of St. John of the Cross.* Living Flame Series, #27. Dublin: Carmelite Center of Spirituality, 1984.

Payne, Steven. *John of the Cross and the Cognitive Value of Mysticism.* Norwell, MA: Kluwer Academic Publishers, 1990.

Peers, E. Allison. *Spirit of Flame: A Study of St. John of the Cross.* Reprint ed. Wilton, CT: Morehouse-Barlow Co., 1979.

Stein, Edith. *The Science of the Cross.* Trans. Josephine Koeppel. Washington, DC: ICS Publications, 1997.

Tavard, George. *Poetry and Contemplation in St. John of the Cross.* Athens, OH: Ohio University Press, 1988.

Thompson, Colin. *The Poet and the Mystic: A Study of the Cántico Espiritual of San Juan de la Cruz.* Oxford, England: Oxford University Press, 1977.

Thompson, William M. *Fire and Light: On Consulting the Saints, Mystics and Martyrs in Theology.* Mahwah, NJ: Paulist Press, 1987. Chaps. 6 & 7.
von Balthasar, Hans Urs. *The Glory of the Lord: A Theological Aesthetics, Vol. III: Studies in Theological Style: Lay Styles,* translated by Andrew Louth et al. San Francisco, CA: Ignatius Press, 1986.
Welch, John. *When Gods Die: An Introduction to John of the Cross.* Mahwah, NJ: Paulist Press, 1990.
Wojtyla, Karol. *Faith According to Saint John of the Cross.* San Francisco, CA: Ignatius Press, 1981.

V. Selected Post-Teresian Figures and Developments

Borriello, Luigi. *Spiritual Doctrine of Elizabeth of the Trinity.* Staten Island, NY: Alba House, 1986.
Carmel in the United States, 1790–1990. By Association of Queen of Carmel. Eugene, OR: Queen's Press, 1990.
Currier, Charles W. *Carmel in America, 1790–1990.* Centennial edition. Darien, IL: Carmelite Press, 1990.
Dickinson, Clare Joseph. *The Carmelite Adventure: Clare Joseph Dickinson's Journal of a Trip to America and Other Documents.* Edited by Constance FitzGerald. Baltimore, MD: Discalced Carmelites, 1990.
Elizabeth of the Trinity. *Complete Works,* Vol. 1: *General Introduction, Major Spiritual Writings.* Trans. Aletheia Kane. Washington, DC: ICS Publications, 1984.
_____. *Complete Works, Vol. 2: Letters from Carmel.* Trans. Anne Englund Nash. Washington, DC: ICS Publications, 1994.
Gil, Czeslaus. *Father Raphael Kalinowski.* Kracow, 1979.
Griffin, Michael, comp. *A New Hymn to God: Saint Teresa of the Andes.* Washington, DC: Teresian Charism Press, 1993
_____. comp. & trans. *Testimonies to Blessed Teresa of the Andes.* Washington, DC: Teresian Charism Press, 1991.
_____, trans. *God the Joy of My Life: A Biography of Saint Teresa of the Andes, with the Saint's* Spiritual Diary. 2d ed. Hubertus, WI: Teresian Charism Press, 1994.
_____, trans. *Letters of Saint Teresa of the Andes.* Hubertus, WI: Teresian Charism Press, 1994.
Kappes, Marcianne. *Track of the Mystic: The Spirituality of Jessica Powers.* Kansas City, MO: Sheed & Ward, 1994.
Lawrence of the Resurrection, Br. *Writings and Conversations on the Practice of the Presence of God.* Critical edition by Conrad De Meester. Trans. by Salvatore Sciurba. Washington, DC: ICS Publications, 1994.
Matthew, Monk. *Saint From the Salt Mines: A Biography of Bd. Raphael Kalinowski.* Oxford, England: Carmelite Book Service, 1986.
Nevin, Winifred. *Heirs of St. Teresa of Avila.* Milwaukee, WI: Bruce, 1959.

Philipon, M. M. *The Spiritual Doctrine of Elizabeth of the Trinity.* reprint. Washington, DC: Teresian Charism Press, 1985.

Poslusney, Venard, trans. and ed. *Prayer, Aspiration and Contemplation: From the Writings of John of St. Samson.* Staten Island, NY: Alba House, 1975.

Rodriguez, Otilio. *A History of the Teresian Carmel.* Darlington, n.d.

Stefanotti, Robert. *The Phoenix of Rennes: The Life and Poetry of John of St. Samson, 1571-1636.* New York: Peter Lang, 1994.

Stein, Edith. *The Hidden Life: Hagiographic Essays, Meditations, Spiritual Texts.* Trans. Waltraut Stein. Washington, DC: ICS Publications, 1992.

_____. *Life in a Jewish Family.* Trans. Josephine Koeppel. Washington, DC: ICS Publications, 1986.

Thérèse of Lisieux. *General Correspondence.* Trans. John Clarke. 2 vols. Washington, DC: ICS Publications, 1982–88.

_____. *Her Last Conversations.* Trans. John Clarke. Washington, DC: ICS Publications, 1977.

_____. *The Poetry of St. Thérèse of Lisieux.* Trans. Donald Kinney. Washington, DC: ICS Publications, 1995.

_____. *Story of a Soul: The Autobiography of St. Thérèse of Lisieux.* Trans. John Clarke. 3d ed. Washington, DC: ICS Publications, 1997.

Valabek, Redemptus Maria, ed. *The Beatification of Father Titus Brandsma, Carmelite (1881–1942): Martyr in Dachau.* Rome: Institutum Carmelitanum, 1986.

_____, ed. *Essays on Titus Brandsma: Carmelite Educator, Journalist, Martyr.* Rome: Institutum Carmelitanum, 1985.

The Institute of Carmelite Studies promotes research and publication in the field of Carmelite spirituality. Its members are Discalced Carmelites, part of a Roman Catholic community—friars, nuns, and laity—who are heirs to the teaching and way of life of Teresa of Jesus and John of the Cross, men and women dedicated to contemplation and to ministry in the church and the world. Information concerning their way of life is available through local diocesan Vocation Offices, or from the Vocation Director's Office, 1525 Carmel Road, Hubertus, WI, 53033.